Remembering
Eckhardt & Haug Ancestors
from
New York City

Remembering Eckhardt & Haug Ancestors from New York City

LOUISE A. ECKHARDT

Genealogy Publishing Group
Amherst, Massachusetts

Published by Genealogy Publishing Group, a division of White River Press
PO Box 3561, Amherst, Massachusetts 01004.
GenealogyPublishingGroup.com

ISBN: 978-1-935052-93-7

Cover Design by Lufkin Graphic Designs
Norwich, Vermont • www.LufkinGraphics.com

Library of Congress Cataloging-in-Publication Data

Names: Eckhardt, Louise A., 1955- author.
Title: Remembering Eckhardt & Haug ancestors from New York City / Louise A.
   Eckhardt.
Description: Amherst, Massachusetts : Genealogy Publishing Group, [2022] |
   Summary: "Narrative profiles of the author's four grandparents and her
   great-aunt, Eva Haug Lenning. They were all German immigrants and Louise
   has combined family photos and stories to give us a personal look at
   immigrant life in New York City in the late nineteenth and early
   twentieth centuries. Includes family trees of each of the five main
   individuals, photos, and documents"-- Provided by publisher.
Identifiers: LCCN 2022045774 | ISBN 9781935052937 (hardcover)
Subjects: LCSH: Eckert family. | Haug family. | German Americans--New York
   (State)--New York--Genealogy. | New York (N.Y.)--Genealogy
Classification: LCC CS71.E1873 2022 | DDC 929/.20973--dc23/eng/20220929
LC record available at https://lccn.loc.gov/2022045774

Dedicated to my parents, Marion and George Eckhardt, who always took such a keen interest in my family history research, encouraged my efforts and patiently answered my endless questions.

Contents

Introduction

It was August 1991 and Hurricane Bob was pummeling the New Jersey shore. As wind and rain beat against the windows my parents and I were stuck inside and glued to the TV. Besides the storm, a coup attempt was underway to unseat the Russian President, Michel Gorbachev. That's why I remember the exact time and place I became interested in family history – but had no idea it would lead to a life-long obsession!

Years earlier my mother had embroidered a beautiful family tree and gave it to me as a gift. I treasured the piece and had it displayed in my living room in a beautiful gold frame. Probably because of that expensive frame, it was stolen in a move and I was sick about the loss. Afterwards, I kept pestering my mother to reconstruct the family information but she was losing her sight by then and could no longer do that kind of needlework.

During that stormy visit, my mother brought out a box full of fragile old photos and documents that I had never seen before. Some of the documents were large baptism and confirmation certificates written in German from as early as the 1870s. My mother gave me everything to take home and my intent was to spend a "few months" and get it all sorted out. Needless to say that was a very unrealistic goal!

Here it is over 30 years later and I'm still trying to sort it all out! From that visit with my parents, I became hooked on family history research and what an interesting and exciting journey it's been! But now that I've accumulated a room full of information and so many interesting stories I decided I'd better try and compile it into something readable. After all, who would want to wade through all my files, notes and notebooks?

This book represents my first attempt to write about my ancestors. I started with my four grandparents but decided to include my great-aunt Eva too. She had written a family history that was invaluable for my research and without her "Henry Haug Story" so much information would have been lost to history. Including her in this book is a way to pay homage to her and her effort to preserve our family history.

Along this journey, I discovered that this kind of writing is more difficult than I had anticipated but also more interesting than I had imagined – especially when you try to place the individual in the context of the time and place they lived. The writing took me 12 years. And had it not been for the corona virus pandemic and being forced to stay inside I might never have finished!

Here are five short profiles about the lives of my four grandparents, Anna and William Eckhardt, Louise and Edward Haug, and my great aunt Eva Lenning. Next, I intend to go back another generation and write about my great-grandparents – because there are so many more stories to tell!

William Eckhardt

The George & Rachel Eckhardt Family

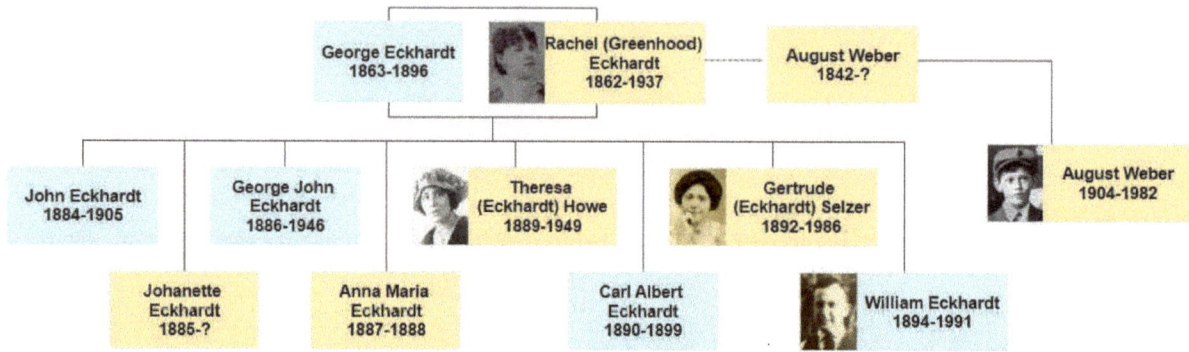

The William & Anna Eckhardt Family

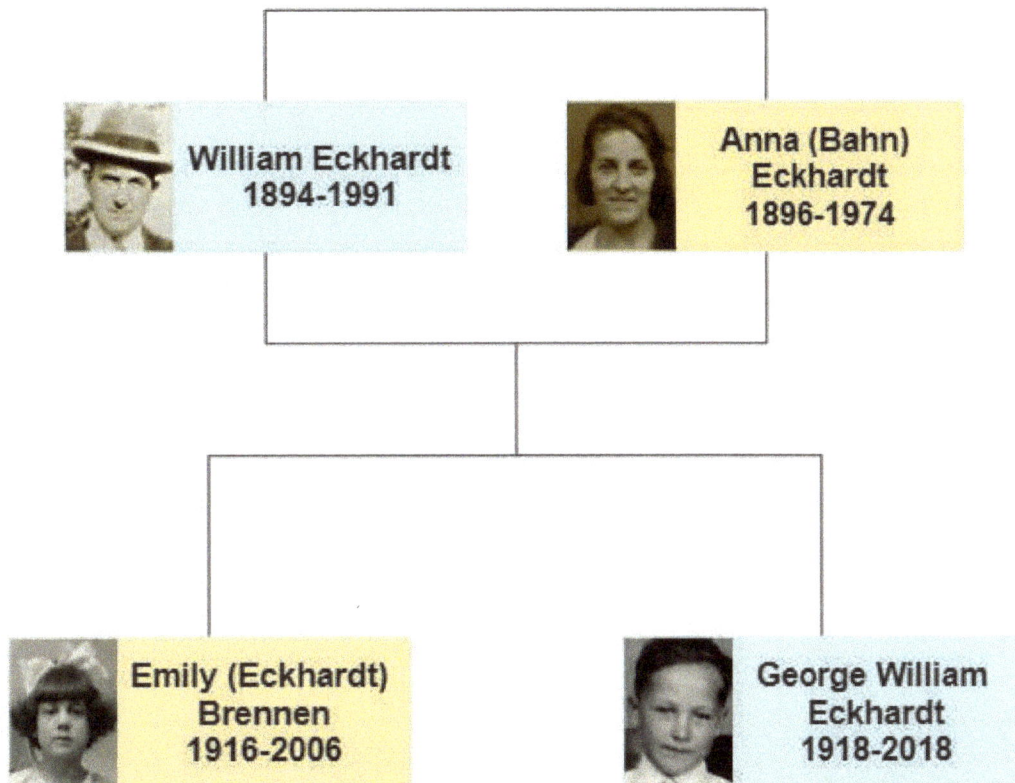

William Eckhardt
1894-1991

Anna (Bahn)
Eckhardt
1896-1974

Emily (Eckhardt)
Brennen
1916-2006

George William
Eckhardt
1918-2018

The William & Anna Eckhardt Family

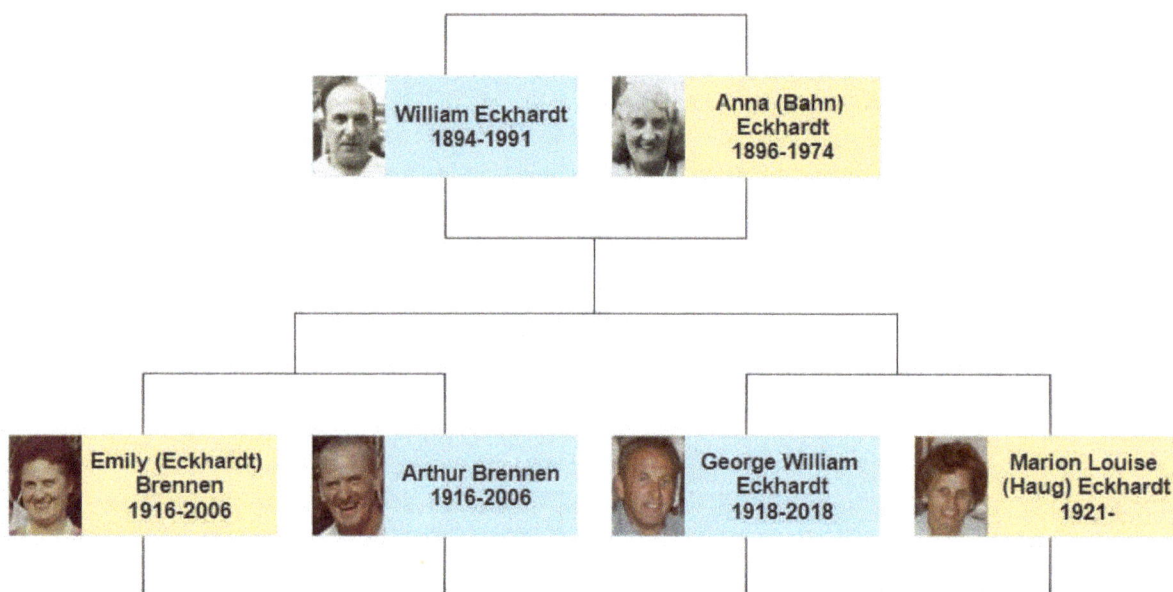

William Eckhardt
1894-1991

Anna (Bahn)
Eckhardt
1896-1974

Emily (Eckhardt)
Brennen
1916-2006

Arthur Brennen
1916-2006

George William
Eckhardt
1918-2018

Marion Louise
(Haug) Eckhardt
1921-

WILLIAM ECKHARDT

It was a very sad and gloomy Christmas for the Eckhardt family in 1896 – with few, if any presents for the six young children. They huddled together in their cold and crowded tenement apartment, frightened and grief-stricken. Rachel, their mother, must have felt the weight of the world on her shoulders as she agonized over how to feed her children and keep a roof over their heads.

My grandfather, William, was the youngest child in that family and hopefully unaware of the tragedy around him. As an adult he would never speak about his childhood. He was a quiet man by nature but even more so about his early years. William's children never knew much about their father's childhood either – just that he had to work at an early age. From around the age of 8, William sold newspapers to help support the family. So many questions I wish I had asked my grandfather before he died in 1991.

What I did know was that William Eckhardt was born in Baltimore, Maryland on July 4, 1894 and lived the rest of his life in Brooklyn, Queens and Long Island, New York.

In time, I learned that George and Rachel (Greenhood) Eckhardt were William's parents, both born in Manhattan, New York City. They were married July 15, 1883 in the Evangelical Reformed Church in lower Manhattan. The family primarily lived in New York City except for about an 8-year period when they lived in Baltimore, Maryland.

The Eckhardt family was involved in the garment industry – which had become central to New York City's economic growth and development. Following the invention of the sewing machine in the 1850s and the accessibility of ready-to-wear clothing, the garment industry exploded – and no place more so than in New York City where newly arrived immigrants could ply their sewing and tailoring skills to earn a living. The garment district had its roots in the Lower East Side of Manhattan starting with tailors doing the work themselves and usually at their homes. In time, they sometimes set up shop with a few employees specializing in different parts of the manufacturing process: designing and buying the fabric, cutting the fabric and the actual sewing.

George Eckhardt was a fabric cutter, a responsible job that could be very costly if one made mistakes. George's older brother, John, also practiced this same skill and both were employed in Baltimore in 1886, according to a Baltimore city directory. A few years later they both returned to New York City where John became quite successful as a manufacturer of women's cloaks. Sadly, George was not as fortunate. In 1896, he died two days before Christmas at the age of 35.

One wonders if little William, only 17 months old at the time, was aware of his father's illness and the sadness in the home. His father had contracted pulmonary tuberculosis – a disease that was all too common in the late 19th century when most inner city families lived in crowded, poorly ventilated tenements. George must have grown weaker and thinner as the disease took its toll. He left behind a widow and six children. The oldest child was 12 and the youngest was my grandfather, William, only 17 months. With no apparent means of income or support who could Rachel turn to for help? Her parents had died and so had her husband's parents. There was no social security system at that time and probably no life insurance policy either. But more sadness was in store for this young family that I did not discover until many years later.

Not much else is known about William's boyhood. However, his son, George Eckhardt, does remember his father talking about the General Slocum disaster – a pleasure boat that sank in the East River in 1904. Over 1,000 people drowned, mostly women and children. William's church, along with other local churches, probably helped with the aftermath since the outing was sponsored by a Lutheran church in the German section of Manhattan. This tragedy occurred when William was a young boy, just 10 years old, and it obviously left a lasting impression on him.

William (seated) with good friend Dick Davis

William did not attend school beyond the 6th grade which was typical at that time. However, he would become an industrious person, always a very hard worker probably borne out of necessity. And he accomplished whatever he set his mind to despite his limited formal education.

By his late teens William was employed as a machine operator with the Robert Gair Company, a manufacturer of paper boxes, printed labels, envelopes and stationary. Located along the East River waterfront between the Brooklyn Bridge and Manhattan Bridge, this area was one of the largest industrial and manufacturing centers in Brooklyn and New York City and is now an historic district. Thousands of workers, including many immigrants, poured into this area every day by ferries, elevated railroads and an extensive transportation network that reached all sections of Brooklyn. They worked in a complex of factories and manufacturing businesses producing a wide variety of goods: machinery, paint, sugar, coffee, packaged groceries, paper boxes and shoes. By 1913, William was one of over 1700 people employed by the Robert Gair Company, a major industry in this teeming district.

Around this time William met a young lady at a dance hall who was attractive and outgoing. William was smitten. Her name was Anna Bahn, the daughter of German immigrants who also lived in the Williamsburg section of Brooklyn. From early photos, one can see why Anna was attracted to this handsome, young man who was a dapper dresser and loved to dance. He usually wore a suit and tie, sometimes a vest, and a bowler or derby hat. About the same

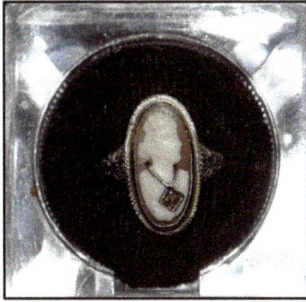

height, William and Anna must have made a handsome couple gliding across the dance floor to popular tunes of the day like, "Let Me Call You Sweetheart," and "You Made Me Love You."

Before long, William proposed and presented Anna with a beautiful cameo and white gold filigree ring as an engagement present. They were married on May 15, 1915, at the Immanuel Lutheran Church on South 9th Street in Brooklyn when William was 21 years old and Anna 18. William's older sister Gertrude and her husband Conrad Selzer were the witnesses – just as William had been a witness at the Selzer marriage three years earlier.

Anna was the love of William's life and their marriage was a long and happy one – for it lasted 59 years until Anna's death in 1974. Even in their mid-70s, they enjoyed dancing and can be seen waltzing proudly at a family affair that has fortunately been preserved on video tape.

Returning to the year 1915, however, the newlyweds initially lived with William's mother, Rachel, and step-brother, August Weber, in their apartment at 203 Middleton Street. "Willy" worked with paper boxes and Anna was a cake wrapper according to the 1915 Brooklyn city census. On the same block was the Gayety Theater where they enjoyed watching burlesque shows with William's mother, older brother George, and sister-in-law Catherine.

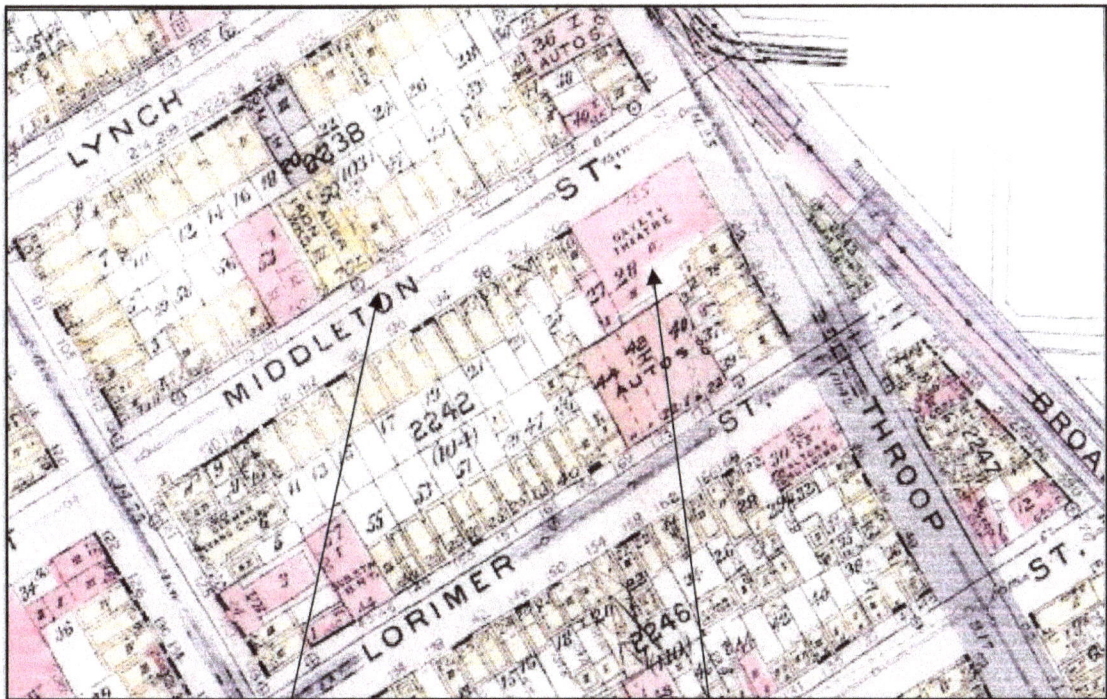

William's mother lived at 203 Middleton Street in Brooklyn from around 1904 until 1935. The family lived in the middle of the block and on the opposite side of the street from the Gayety Theatre.

Gayety Theatre, Brooklyn, N. Y.

Gayety Theatre, circa 1908. (Photo and program courtesy of B. Merlis, www.Brooklynpix.com)

GAYETY THEATRE
The Home of Vaudeville and Burlesque

HYDE & BEHMAN AMUSEMENT CO.   Proprietors
JAMES J. CLARK   Manager

Matinee Daily 2:15   Evenings 8:15

BROADWAY AND THROOP AVENUE

Soon Willy and Anna were able to move to their own apartment several blocks away at 50 Devoe Street but still relatively close to their parents. How happy they must have been with the arrival of their first child in December 1916. They named her Emily after Anna's mother, Emilia.

But a war brewing in Europe was a continuous worry. Although President Wilson had pledged U.S. neutrality in 1914, he severed diplomatic relations with the German Empire in 1917 following submarine attacks on U.S. vessels. On April 2, 1917, President Wilson delivered his War Message before a Special Session of Congress and four days later Congress overwhelmingly passed the War Resolution against the Central Powers in Europe. The United States had entered the Great War.

William was one of 24 million men who registered for military service during World War I. On June 5, 1917, William went to his local Brooklyn precinct in to sign up in the first wave of registrations for all men between the ages of 21 and 31. He was 23 years old at the time, married with one child, and still working as a machinist with the Robert Gair Company on Washington Street in Brooklyn. According to his registration card, William was a tall man of medium build with brown eyes and brown hair who had not lost any arms, legs, hands, etc. Due to a heart murmur though, William did not serve in World War I.

William's World War I Registration with his birth year incorrectly annotated as 1893 instead of 1894.

By January 1920, the family was now living on Locust Street, Brooklyn. This address was closer to the bus and streetcar lines that William probably used to go to work along the East River waterfront. There was also a new addition to the household – baby George whose age was recorded as "1 year and 5/12" in the 1920 U.S. census, along with his sister Emily who was "2 and 10/12." William was working as a machinist with envelopes.

Anna and William with baby Emily born December 23, 1916 (left). Their second child, George, was born August 8, 1918.

The 1920s were a busy time for the Eckhardt family. On November 28, 1920, William and Anna purchased a 30' x 100' lot in South Ozone Park, Queens – next door to William's sister, Theresa. Harry and Theresa Howe, with their children, William and Daisy, purchased their lot on the same day. South Ozone Park was a very rural area at the time with many farms in the local area. The lot was atop a hill surrounded by woods with lots of rabbits. Next to them was a vacant lot and George said you could see all the way down to Jamaica Bay. A road had been carved out of the hill but it was not paved for many years – no gas, electric or sewers at first either.

Little Emily and George had many playmates and lots of freedom to run around and explore. In summer they would pick big, juicy tomatoes from the local farms or wild berries in the woods. In winter, they had fun sleigh-riding down their driveway, across the road and straight down the steep hill.

William built the house in Queens himself – an amazing feat considering he had very little money, no car and no knowledge or experience building a home. But he studied other houses and figured out how to go about it. Working outside, often in frigid temperatures, William worked steadily hand-carrying all the materials from Brooklyn by train and trolley. Anna helped dig the foundation for the house that eventually stood on locust posts. As the house started to take shape, the family lived in one room while the construction continued.

Building the house in South Ozone Park, Queens.

While William was at work, George, then a teen-ager, mixed the mortar and helped two workmen with all the brickwork. He remembers a furnace in the cellar with a grate in the floor above that he would stand on for a blast of warm air. One time one of the gas lamps in the house exploded and everyone had to dash outside, but William was able to extinguish the fire in the nick of time.

The finished home at 133-44 123rd St. built by William with help from his son George.

Eventually William succeeded in building a one-story, three-bedroom brick home with a garage underneath and a large stoop in front. Conditions were pretty primitive at first with an outhouse and kerosene lighting – but in time, electricity, plumbing and heating were installed and the city ran sewer lines above ground. Several years later, George installed garage doors. This house still stands today, at 133-44 123rd Street near JFK Airport in South Ozone Park, Queens.

On Black Tuesday, October 29, 1929, the stock market crashed – the start of the Great `Depression. By this time, Gair Company had moved out of New York City, but William was fortunate to find other employment at Bush Terminal on the Brooklyn waterfront. As a result, the Eckhardts fared pretty well during the Depression with enough to eat, but few luxuries.

However, it was many years before the Eckhardts could afford to buy a car. In the meantime, William had a long walk and then a long commute to work – but he was not alone. One of the family dogs would usually follow him to the train station and then find his way home again.

William at work as a paper adjuster

Working long hours, Wiliam seldom made it home before 7:00 PM and then the family would sit down to eat dinner.

By 1930, William and Anna were 34 and 33 years old and the proud owners of a home valued at $5,000. They also owned a "radio set" according to the 1930 census. William was an adjuster in a paper factory and Emily and George, ages 13 and 11, both attended Public School 46 in Queens.

In the 1930s, William and Anna bought another lot, this time at Lake Ronkonkoma, Long Island. They had a small bungalow built next to the Fisher family since their daughter Emily and Muriel Fisher were best friends back in Queens. Here the Eckhardts enjoyed summer vacations at the Lake and Emily and George palled around with lots of kids who would become life-long friends. They also had teenage romances that would have happy endings with marriages that lasted over 60 years.

William and Anna at Lake Ronkonkoma

The late 1930s and early 1940s marked the rise of Adolph Hitler and the beginning of another World War. On September 23, 1940, President Franklin Roosevelt initiated the Selective Service System – the first peacetime draft in U.S. history. By the war's end almost 51 million men would register in one of seven registrations.

The fourth registration took place in April, 1942 and applied to William and all men born between 28 April 1877 and 16 February 1897. Notices like this one in *The New York Times* appeared in local newspapers, "All Men 45-64 Required to Register at Week-End." Often called the "old men's registration" those who registered were never intended for military service; this was more of an occupational survey in case their skills were required for the war effort.

Men were eager to sign up and their enthusiasm made front-page news in *The New York Times*: "269,100 Older Men In Early Rush Here For Draft Listing . . . Draft Boards in Metropolitan Area Report Eagerness To Contribute To War." By the second day, the Local Boards were flooded and needed additional volunteers as registrars. As reported by *The New York Times* on Monday, April 27, 1942, ". . . the average waiting time ran about an hour in mid-afternoon. However, everyone seemed cheerful and good-natured as the lines moved slowly ahead into the vacant stores, school houses and fire houses that served as registration places . . . Men came equipped with camp chairs or stools on which they sat and chatted with their neighbors . . ." *The New York Daily News* ran a story on the same day, "68,000 Clerks Kept On Go As Grandpas' Rush To Sign" and noted that men were not the only ones on line. "Remarkable about yesterday's registration was the large number of women in the lines – not to register, of course, but to chat with their husbands during the wait."

William registered on the first day, Saturday, April 25th, 1942, at Local Board 280 in Queens. By then he was 47 years old and employed by the Oneida Paper Company at 601 West 26th Street in Manhattan. William worked there several years until he was derailed by a very serious injury. He had shattered disks in his back – probably from lifting big, heavy rolls of paper into the machines at work. During back surgery, a bone was grafted from his leg to his back which left a 10" incision in his leg and gave him more problems than his back did. His son, George, remembers his father hobbling to the grocery store and tying his bundles onto his crutches. William was out of work for 2 ½ years recuperating from 1943 to 1945. He probably received compensation since he had sustained a work-related injury.

William's World War II ration book

In 1945, William narrowly missed another catastrophic accident. At their summer bungalow, he lit a cigarette in the outhouse and was blown out the door by an explosion. Gasoline was stored in the outhouse and there must have been a leak in one of the cans that ignited when William struck a match. Fortunately, the next door neighbor, Mrs. Fisher, was close by. She rushed to the rescue and applied oil to William's burned face. Had the door not been closed his injuries probably would have been much worse.

William returned to work by the end of 1946 but shortly afterwards, Oneida Paper Products moved to California. The company asked him to move as well, but he declined.

According to Social Security records, William worked for three different paper products companies in 1948. Then he landed a job at Samuel Cupples Envelope Company, Inc. at 360 Furman Street in Brooklyn. Except for time off in 1952 for cataract surgery, William worked at Samuel Cupples from 1949 until his retirement in 1955 at the age of 61. And then he and Anna were free to fulfill their retirement dreams.

By February 1954, the Eckhardts had sold their bungalow at Lake Ronkonkoma after many years of enjoyment. Just one month later, they purchased wooded lots in Babylon, Long Island, near their daughter Emily who was living in Massapequa Park. Their son, George, who was a building inspector in New York City, designed a home for his parents. William hired contractors to build the house and then finished the interior, and the patio and landscaping with George's help. It turned out to be a cozy two-bedroom home with a garage and a lovely lawn in the front and back. By summer 1955, the Eckhardts had sold their home in Queens and moved to Long Island to begin the next chapter of their lives.

House under construction at 295 Neptune Ave., North Babylon, New York

The year 1955 is also when I entered the picture – the daughter of George and Marion Eckhardt and granddaughter of William and Anna. I loved my grandparents dearly but going to visit them when I was a kid was a trial. That's because I got carsick – so the 90 minute drive was endless and I usually arrived in the horizontal position looking slightly green.

The author on a visit to Grandma and Grandpa's house

But I can still see my grandfather waiting for us to arrive – sitting in the garage with a cap on and puffing away on his cigar. And when I began to recover, he always had an ice cream bar ready for me and talked about sarsaparilla and tutti-frutti soda with a twinkle in his eye.

We would sometimes go for a walk along the country roads, my grandfather, my father and me. I remember there were few other homes in the area – mostly woods with rabbits, squirrels and other small animals. It was very quiet and peaceful except for our voices and the sound of our shoes scuffling along the sandy roads. We would also have family get-togethers at my grandparent's house to celebrate the 4th of July – most appropriate, of course, since my grandfather was born on the 4th of July. How exciting it was to watch the firecrackers sizzle and shoot into the sky with a booming sound and an explosion of color.

My grandparents took great pride in their home and it was immaculate inside and out. They had beautiful flowers and my grandfather always kept the lawn manicured and the bushes neatly trimmed. And I remember my grandmother's delight in watching the birdbath out front and her concern that the birds always have fresh water to drink and a cool place to take a dip.

I loved it when my grandparents came to visit us on Staten Island and stayed overnight. I'd wake up early and pester my parents until they would let me go in and visit my grandmother. I'd climb in bed with her and she would tell me the most wonderful stories. My grandfather, however, was nowhere in sight. He always got up much earlier, walked to a local bakery and brought back fresh "crullers" for breakfast and warm bread with delicious globs of cinnamon in the center.

I have one other memory of my grandfather when I was a child that I had completely forgotten. It came back to me many years later as if someone thumped me on the head while I was driving. I remembered a day at Jones Beach on Long Island, NY, when my grandfather took me to the playground on the boardwalk. I got a splinter in my foot so he carried me back down to the beach to rejoin my parents. Somewhere along the way I asked him if he would go swimming in the ocean and he said he would not. He'd had a brother who drowned and therefore, never learned to swim.

John Eckhardt's death certificate. May 23. 1905

To this day I have no idea why I remembered that long-forgotten snippet of conversation. But it gave me a clue about my grandfather's childhood – one that even my father and Aunt Emily were unaware of. So I followed the trail.

In time I was able to confirm my grandfather's story. I found a 1905 death certificate for John Eckhardt, who was 22 years old when he drowned in the East River. He was a tailor living with his mother and siblings at 203 Middleton St. How tragic – and to think William was only 10 years old when his elder brother died. What a painful experience for him and the rest of his family.

According to an article in *The Brooklyn Citizen* newspaper, May 24, 1905, John "drowned a week ago last Sunday while fishing from the recreation pier at the foot of North Second street pier." A boat captain saw the body being carried along by the current near the North Twelfth street pier and secured it with a boat hook. "His mother, Rachel Eckhardt, had passed sleepless nights and was sitting at a front window when a policeman apprised her of the finding of the body."

William had another brother who also died tragically. Charles Eckhardt died July 11, 1899, of a "coma following septicemia subsequent to inclusion of knee joint – tubercular abscess." He was only 8 years old.

Charles's place of death, as well as his last place of residence, was 155 Worth St. according to his death certificate. This is significant because the Five Points House of Industry was located at 155 Worth St. It was described as a home for the "preservation of children from crime and destitution." "The institution also boards children of poor parents at merely nominal rates; shelters women while they are seeking work as servants; and affords temporary relief to destitute families in its neighborhood" as stated in an 1892 Handbook of New York City.

Death certificate for Charles Eckhardt, July 11, 1899

Infirmary of the Five Points House of Industry at 155 Worth Street in Manhattan where Charles Eckhardt died. (Photo from King's Handbook of New York City, 1892)

William's two sisters were also "inmates" at the Five Points House of Industry according to the 1900 census. Theresa was 12 years old and Gertrude 7 and both were attending school. Following the death of her husband, Rachel must have been financially desperate and had no alternative but to place three of her children in this home.

Index cards from the 1900 U.S. population census showing William's sisters both living at The Five Points House of Industry.

Research gives a much clearer picture as to why William never spoke about his early years. He faced so many tragedies as a young boy. The illness and early death of William's father must have left this family of seven in dire straits. The two older boys, John and George, had to work to provide income while Rachel kept William at home since he was just a baby. It must have been a gut-wrenching decision for Rachel to place her three middle children in a home – Charlie, Theresa and Gertrude – and Charlie died there in 1899. Even William worked as a young boy selling newspapers to bring in extra income for the family. Then William's brother drowned in 1905. However, one positive note in an otherwise sad story is that the girls appear to have left the home by 1905 for the family was once again living together at 203 Middleton Street, according to the city census of that year.

Anna and William's 50th anniversary, May 1965 with son George (in the middle), daughter Emily and son-in-law Arthur Brennen and granddaughter Louise

William was very close to his mother until her death in 1935. He and his siblings visited her often when she was hospitalized at Creedmore State Hospital for the last year and a half of her life. William was also close to his two sisters, Theresa Howe and Gertrude Selzer, his brother George and step-brother August Weber. Sadly, George committed suicide in 1947 after suffering from throat cancer.

Although William had a rough start in life, he overcame adversity and lived a long and productive life. He and Anna were happily married for 59 years and worked very hard all their lives. William was largely self- taught but resourceful and progressive. He built his first house and owned three homes during his lifetime – and took great pride in each of them. William was always a solid and dependable family man and an excellent provider even during difficult times. He was a kind-hearted person who was very loyal and dedicated to his family.

William died March 18, 1991, at the age of 96 and is buried beside his wife, Anna, at Cypress Hills Cemetery in Brooklyn, New York.

Anna (Bahn) Eckhardt

The Edward & Emilie Bahn Family

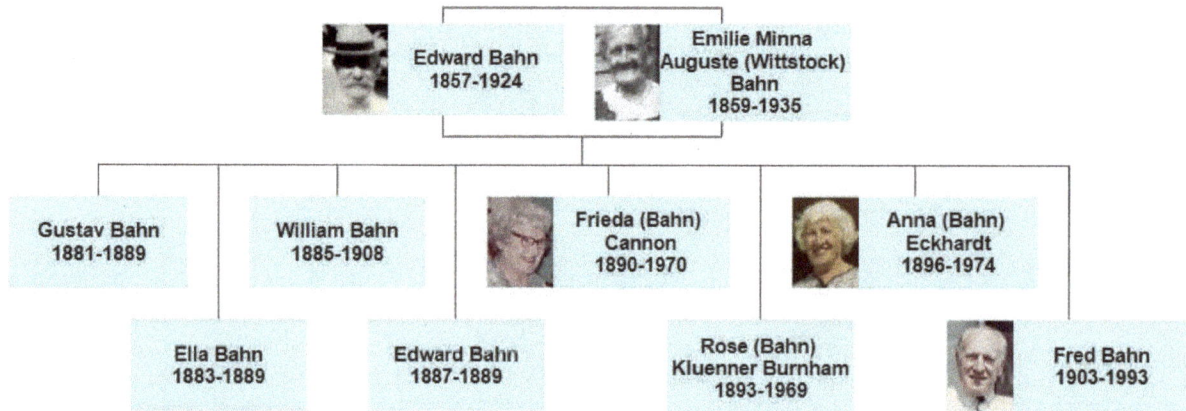

The William & Anna Eckhardt Family

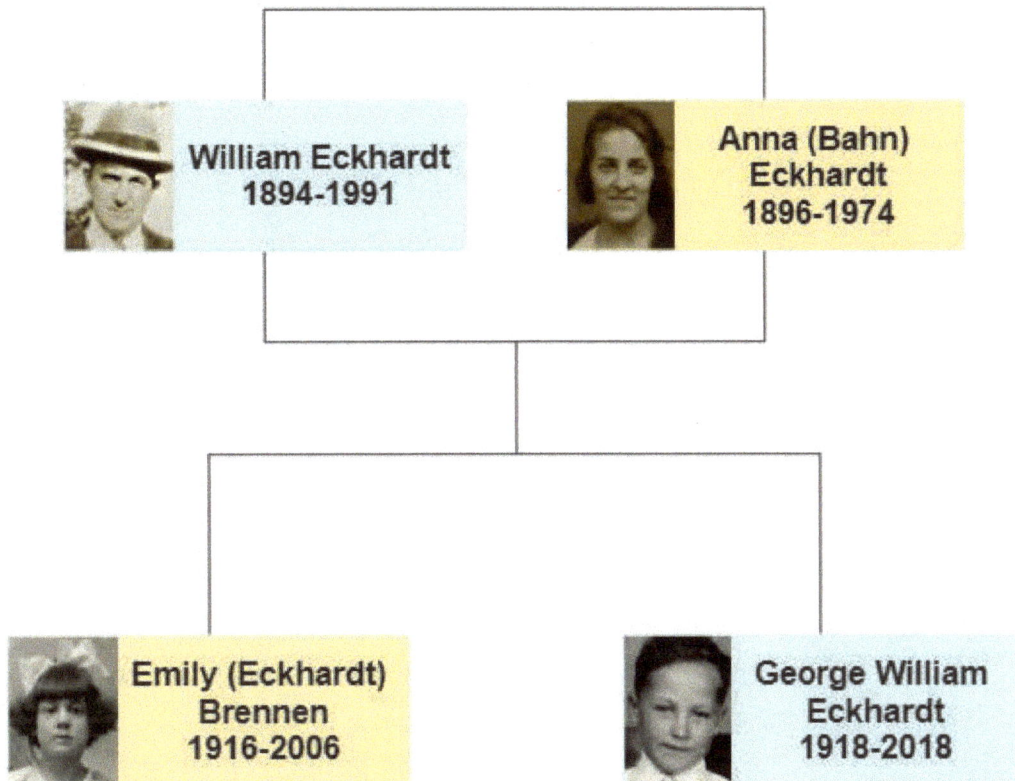

William Eckhardt
1894-1991

Anna (Bahn)
Eckhardt
1896-1974

Emily (Eckhardt)
Brennen
1916-2006

George William
Eckhardt
1918-2018

The William & Anna Eckhardt Family

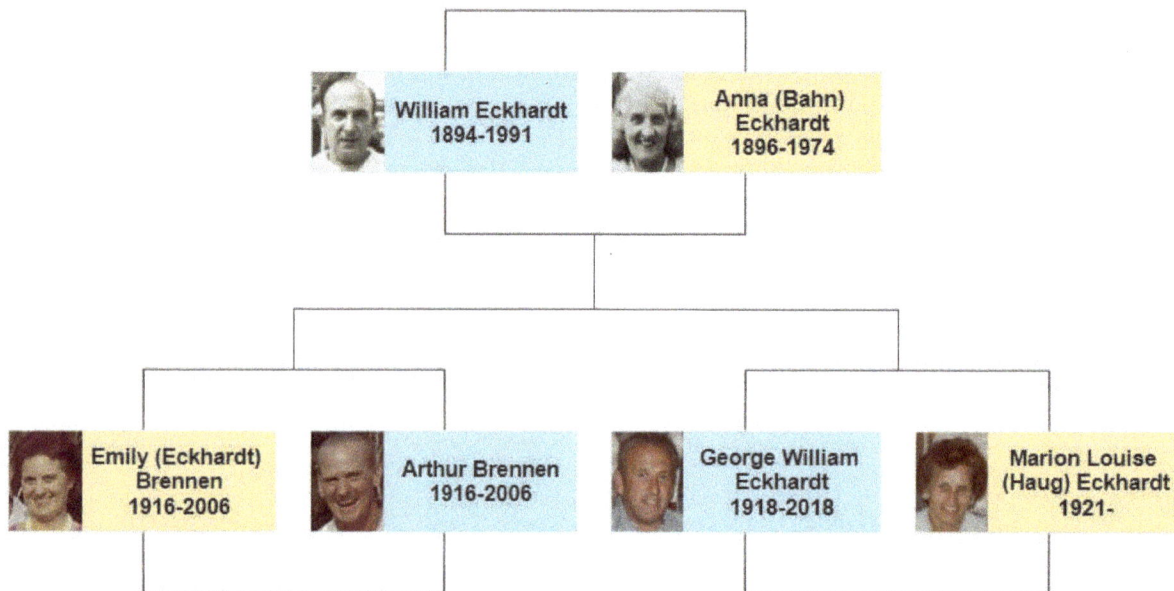

William Eckhardt 1894-1991

Anna (Bahn) Eckhardt 1896-1974

Emily (Eckhardt) Brennen 1916-2006

Arthur Brennen 1916-2006

George William Eckhardt 1918-2018

Marion Louise (Haug) Eckhardt 1921-

Anna Bahn Eckhardt

"We're movie stars," she shouted out the window of the stagecoach as the horses clip-clopped through the congested streets of New York City. Laughing and waving to total strangers, she had had a wonderful day – probably one of the best days of her life. The year was 1969 so this was an unlikely scene in mid-Manhattan – and it's one of the most vivid memories I have of my grandmother, Anna Eckhardt.

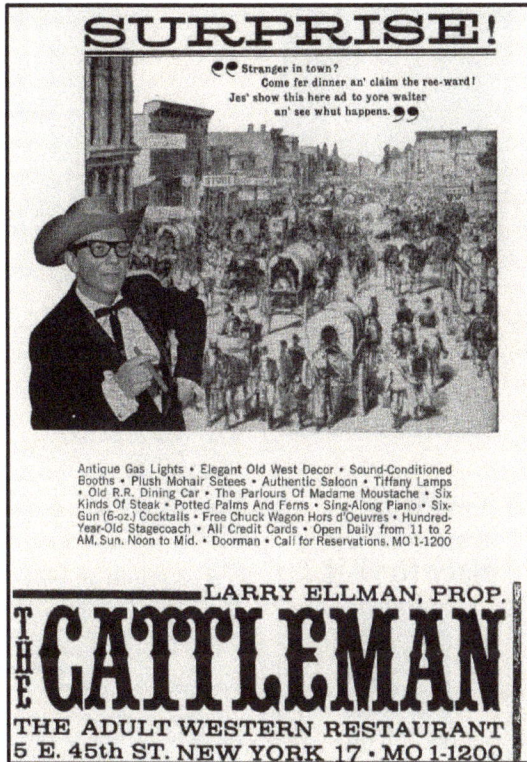

It was my 14th birthday and my mother, grand-mother, aunt, cousin and three girlfriends went to the city to see *Cabaret*, the play starring Joel Gray. The play was terrific, although somewhat risqué, to my mother's dismay. Afterwards, we ate dinner at Cattleman's Restaurant and my grandmother had a grand time laughing and flirting with the waiters. Then we all piled into and on top of a stagecoach that was parked out front and rode around the streets of Manhattan. What a thrill – a perfect day and no one enjoyed it more than my grandmother. And that is how I remember her – as someone who enjoyed people, laughed easily and was always ready to go out and have a good time.

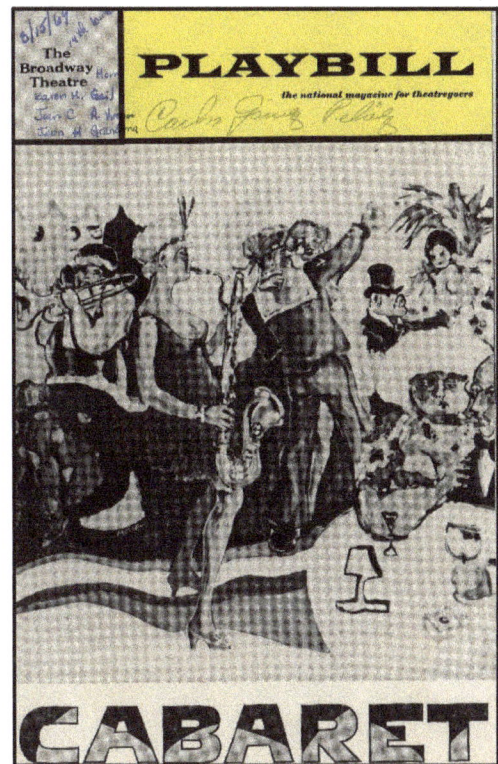

And oh, how Anna loved music!

My father told me many times how his mother, Anna, loved to play the piano and although she had no formal training, she could play by ear. When she heard a tune, she would sit down, pick out the melody and then play it with both hands and with gusto! She also loved to make up songs, especially marches.

She was a very loyal fan of the Lawrence Welk television show and faithfully wrote to Mr. Welk for many years, as well as Myron Floren, the accordion player. (No doubt she told them both about my brother who was also playing the accordion, and so was yours truly, but not with the same enthusiasm).

For my grandmother and me, Radio City Music Hall was a magical place and an exciting journey from Staten Island! We would get up at the crack of dawn, catch a bus to the Staten Island ferry and then a subway to uptown Manhattan. We stood on line and when the doors opened, we'd race down to the front row so we could see the amazing, high-kicking Rockettes up close and listen to the magnificent organ recital that preceded the show. At that time, there was both a movie and an elaborate show. On one of our trips to Radio City, Debbie Reynolds was starring in "The Unsinkable Molly Brown," a movie that broke box-office records for attendance. It was 1964, and despite the summer heat that year, 21,000 people per day stood on a line that wrapped all the way around the building. And somewhere towards the front of that line, my grandmother and I were impatiently waiting to go in.

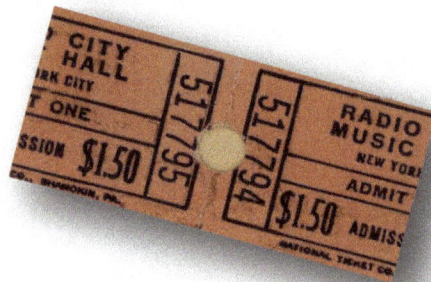

We sat through the show and movie three times! And by the third time, the Rockettes smiled and winked at us. They recognized the little girl and her grandmother with the snow-white hair sitting in the front row. We had no time for lunch, however, so we ate popcorn and candy all day long.

When we arrived home, it was very late and my mother had been pacing the floor with worry. My grandmother and I were both in hot water but as far as I was concerned, it had been a great adventure and my grandmother was loads of fun.

Radio City Music Hall Auditorium   New York City

I have many fond memories of both my Grandma and Grandpa Eckhardt. I loved it when they would visit and stay over. My grandfather always got up very early and walked to the bakery for crullers and cinnamon bread, which were delicious! And I would crawl into bed with my grandmother (after I carefully carried her eyeglasses over from the dresser) and she would tell me wonderful stories about growing up in Brooklyn. But oh how I wish I had asked her more questions about her childhood and her family!

Her parents were German but where they were born was a mystery to me for many years. But eventually I learned that Anna's parents, Edward and Emilie (Wittstock) Bahn, were German-speaking immigrants who had arrived at the port of Baltimore in November, 1883, with two very young children. They made the crossing in steerage and traveled with all their worldly possessions in just one suitcase.

Edward was born October 21, 1857, in Neuenberg, West Prussia, (now known as the town of Nowe in northwestern Poland) and baptized in a Lutheran church. He was the son of Friedrich Bahn, a bricklayer, and Veronica Bartknecht. According to family lore, Edward had been in the German cavalry, rode a white horse and had been stationed in Berlin. He was assigned to a military unit that was legendary for being very daring and brave; they wore a skull and cross bones on their hats. In Brooklyn, Edward was a tinsmith and later worked in the Domino sugar refinery. His grandchildren remember him as having a gray handlebar mustache and very blue eyes.

Edward's wife, Emilie Wittstock Bahn, was born September 30, 1859, in Pasewalk, a small town in northeastern Germany close to the Baltic Sea and the Polish border. Her parents were Franz Wittstock, a trader in Pasewalk, and Wilhelmine Rathsburg. Sadly, both of Emilie's parents died when she was just a child. Her father died of consumption in 1867 at the age of 47, and her mother died in 1874 of uterine cancer at the age of 45.

Anna spoke lovingly of her parents. She described her mother, Emilie, as a very gentle and kind-hearted person who enjoyed sitting in her Morris chair in the living room with a pet chicken in her lap. She adored animals and had a beautiful Collie named Tootsie that could guide her down to the cellar for coal after she lost her sight.

How Edward Bahn and Emilie Wittstock met is lost to history but they were married February 11, 1883 in Neuenberg, West Prussia, and it was believed to be Emilie's second marriage. They were the parents of 12 children but sadly, only four lived to adulthood.

Born September 11, 1896, Anna was the couple's 8th child, according to her birth certificate. (Later paperwork, however, said her birth date was September 10th). The family was living at 8 Stagg Street in the Williamsburg section of Brooklyn which was a very German section at the time. Anna had two older sisters, Frieda and Rose, and the three of them would sing together on Saturday mornings when they did their chores

Not much is known about Anna's childhood except what can be gleaned from local newspapers. Anna and her sister Frieda, for example, were mentioned in *The Daily Standard Union* as having attended "the first package party and dance of the Progressive Literary Circle" held in New Liberty Hall on Thanksgiving Eve, 1907. And on October 7, 1911, Anna played a piano solo at the 8th annual concert at Midwood Hall in Flatbush. It was a very "enjoyable musicale" with about 500 people in attendance according to an article in *The Brooklyn Daily Eagle.*

Although she was still a young child, one can imagine Anna being swept up in the tremendous excitement surrounding the opening of the Williamsburg Bridge in December, 1903. The largest suspicion bridge in the world at the time, the Williamsburg Bridge spanned the East River connecting the Lower East Side of Manhattan with the Williamsburg neighborhood of Brooklyn where the Bahn family lived. As the *New York Times* reported, "the Mayor pronounced the new Williamsburg Bridge open to the public amid the thunder of cannon and the cheers of a vast multitude of enthusiastic people." A huge American flag was unfurled on each end of the tower and the crowds cheered uproariously as numerous bands marched through the streets. The celebration also included a marine pageant of 141 vessels in the East River and continued at night with illumination of the bridge, fireworks, rockets, and bombs that burst in midair and discharged fire that fell in brilliant colors. It must have been a magnificent sight and an exhilarating day! Enormous crowds had lined the waterfront to view the spectacle and it is likely that Anna and her family were somewhere in that crowd enjoying the activities.

Geo. C. Tilyou's Steeplechase—Funny Place
Natures Freaks.

Around this same time, New Yorkers looking to escape the stifling heat and their crowded living conditions flocked to Coney Island in Brooklyn, the largest amusement park in the United States. Besides the beach, Coney Island offered a myriad of rides and exhibits, fireworks and sideshows. I remember my grandmother telling me about sideshow performers who were referred to as "human oddities" or "freaks" at the time and how sad it was to converse with them. But overall, Coney Island, and especially Steeplechase, which was a 15-acre park within Coney Island, was a wonderland full of entertainment. I too have wonderful memories of Coney Island and I know my grandmother did as well.

The year 1909 heralded two other important events. In January, Anna's oldest sister, Frieda, married a baker from Germany and after a brief church ceremony, the family had a small celebration at their home at 378 Stagg Street.

Later in the year, from numerous newspaper accounts, it seems all of New York City and New Jersey were involved in an elaborate, two-week commemoration of Henry Hudson's and Robert Fulton's maritime achievements. Historical and carnival parades took place between September 25, and October 9, 1909, and over 1,000 vessels of all kinds participated in a naval parade. Churches and schools were involved, buildings were decorated, stores closed – there was even a Children's Day, on Saturday, October 2nd. Several hundred thousand children participated in the Hudson-Fulton festival with plays, pageants, floats, concerts and period costumes depicting the history of New York. Anna was 13 years old so it must have been an exciting time for her.

By 1910, the family had moved several times within the same Williamsburg neighborhood. They were now living at 328 Stagg St. According to the federal census of that year, Anna's father was working as a tinsmith at a sugar refinery. Anna's older sister, Rosie, was a packer in a candy factory. Anna wasn't working yet so she was probably responsible for minding her younger brother, Fred, who was 7 years old.

However, a week after her birthday, in September, 1910, Anna received her working papers from the Department of Health. She was now qualified for employment in "any Manufacturing, Mercantile or other establishment in the city." According to that paperwork, she was 5'2", 106 pounds and 14 years old.

Coincidentally, Anna was also baptized the same day she received her working papers. It's puzzling why she wasn't baptized as an infant. Nevertheless, on September 19, 1910, Anna was baptized at the German Evangelical Mission Church (at 151 Leonard and Stagg Streets). Later in life, at the age of 35, she was very proud to be confirmed at St. John's Lutheran Church in Brooklyn.

I remember my grandmother being quite religious. In a thank-you letter to my parents following my confirmation, for example, she wrote, "I was so glad to be in church to sing and pray and take some of the sins off my chest and most of all taking the Lords supper; it was something I longed to do." My father said his family never ate meat on Fridays and that his mother faithfully read her Bible, especially during Lent and Easter.

My sheep hear my voice. John 10.27.

Suffer little Children to come unto me, and forbid them not: For of such is the Kingdom of God. St. Luke 16. 18.

Matth. 23, 37.

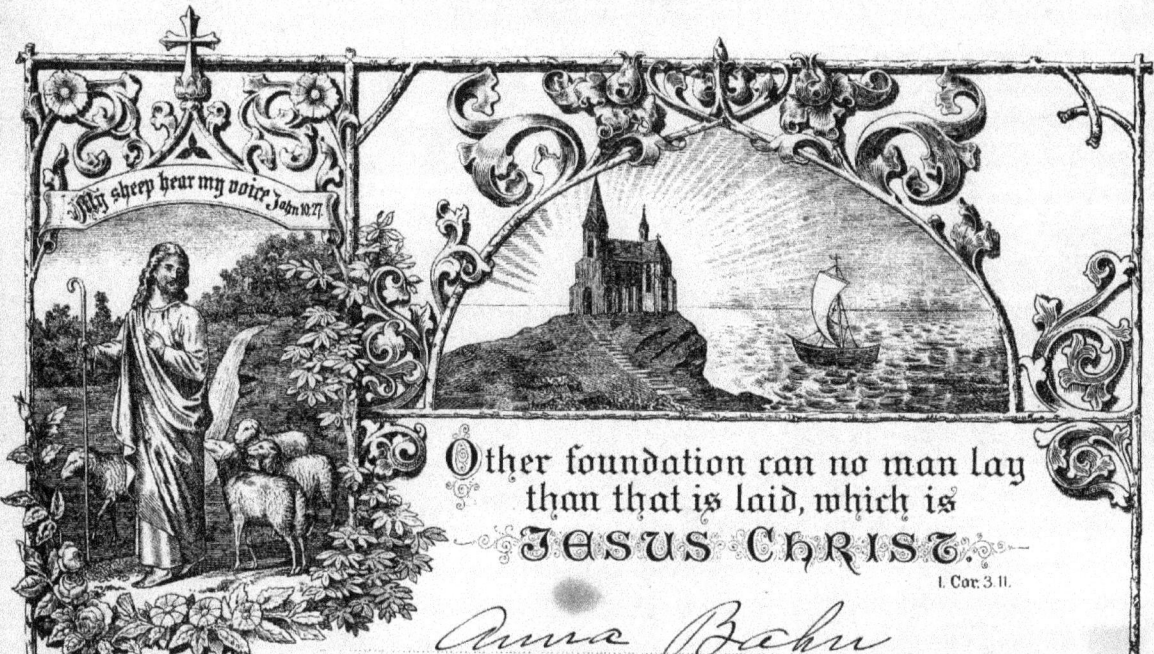

Other foundation can no man lay than that is laid, which is JESUS CHRIST.
I. Cor. 3. 11.

Anna Bahn

Child of Mr. Edward Bahn

and his wife Emilie Bahn née Wittstock

born at Brooklyn N.Y. Sept. 10, 1896

was baptized at Brooklyn N.Y. Sept. 19, 1910

IN THE NAME OF
THE FATHER, OF THE SON AND
OF THE HOLY GHOST

Sponsors were:

Pastor
151 Leonard St.
Brooklyn
N.Y.

Behold the Lamb of God, which taketh away the sin of the world. John 1. 29.

Nº 33.

Published by Ernst Kaufmann, Lahr, Baden
22 & 24 North William Street, NEW YORK.

During the next decade, Anna's world changed dramatically. She met a young man at a dance hall who was charming, a marvelous dancer and a dapper dresser besides. William Eckhardt (or "Willy") as Anna called him, also lived in the Williamsburg section of Brooklyn and had a similar German background. They fell in love and William asked Anna to be his bride with a beautiful cameo ring that I still have today. On May 14, 1915, the couple applied for a marriage license and the very next day they were married at the Immanuel Evangelical Lutheran Church on South 9th Street. The witnesses were William's sister and brother-in-law, Gertrude and Conrad Selzer. Anna was just 18 years old at the time and William was 21 but it was the beginning of a marriage that would last almost 60 years.

Gayety Theatre.   Brooklyn.   N. Y.

At first, the couple lived with William's mother and younger brother at 203 Middleton Street in Williamsburg, as recorded in the 1915 city census. Just down the street was the Gayety Theater which featured high class burlesque and variety acts with well-known entertainers of the day like Will Rogers, Buster Keaton and Phil Silvers. Williams's mother enjoyed attending this theater so it's likely that Anna and William accompanied her as well. Perhaps the newlyweds had not yet had chance to find a place of their own or maybe they could not afford one. Nevertheless, both Anna and William were working: Anna as a candy wrapper, and William as a machine operator.

As I write this, the United States and the world are in the grip of a horrible pandemic of the COVID-19 virus that has killed over 100,000 Americans so far. New York City is the epicenter of the virus, hit harder than any other region of the country. And so it was in 1916 as well, with the outbreak of the polio epidemic. In June, 1916, *The Brooklyn Daily Eagle* officially announced the existence of the epidemic with 24 cases in Brooklyn neighborhoods, including Williamsburg.

Widespread panic ensued, and then, as now, thousands fled the city, public gatherings were canceled and families were quarantined in their homes. So it must have been with a mixture of joy and fear when Anna learned she was expecting her first child.

On December 23, 1916, Anna gave birth to a healthy baby girl and named her Emily, after Anna's mother, Emilie. But she must have continued to worry; polio mainly affected infants and children under age 5 and was known as infantile paralysis, the crippler of children.

Meanwhile, the drumbeat of war in Europe was growing louder and threatening to spill over to the United States. Since the beginning of the war, the U.S. had pursued a policy of neutrality and non-intervention and President Woodrow Wilson had won a narrow victory in 1916 with his campaign slogan, "He kept us out of war." But after Germany resumed unrestricted submarine warfare, sank 7 U.S. merchant ships, and invited Mexico to become an ally against the United States, President Wilson felt compelled to change course. On April 6, 1917, the United States declared was against Germany.

Congress signed the 1917 Selective Service Act into law which authorized the federal government to raise a national army for service in World War I. To relieve the exhausted men on the battlefields in Europe, all men in the United States between the ages of 21 and 30 were now required to register for military service.

That included my grandfather, William Eckhardt. And how Anna must have worried. On June 5, 1917, William signed up at his local precinct in Brooklyn in the first wave of registrations.

With baby Emily, Anna and William were now living in an apartment at 50 Devoe Street in Brooklyn. William was 23 years old and working as a machinist at Robert Gair, a very large company that made paper bags and corrugated fiberboard shipping containers.

Several months later, Anna found out she was going to give birth to a second child. But once again, the joyous news must have been mixed with apprehension for the young couple. The 1918 Spanish flu was raging and became one of the deadliest pandemics in human history. It lasted from the spring of 1918 until spring/summer the following year. And according to historian John M. Barry, "those most likely to die – were pregnant women. Of the pregnant women who did survive childbirth, over 25 percent lost the child." Despite these grim statistics, a healthy baby boy entered the world on August 8, 1918. His parents named him George (after William's father); however, they named him William on his birth certificate! My father was completely unaware of this mix-up until he was drafted into WW II many years later and had a tough time getting the paperwork straightened out.

The Eckhardt Family, 1921

Three months after George was born, World War I ended and Germany signed a ceasefire on the 11th hour of the 11th day of the 11th month. Fortunately, William had not had to serve, probably because he had a heart murmur.

What a turbulent decade the 1910s had been – for the country and for my grandparents!

By 1920, William, Anna and their two children were living at 15 Locust Street in Brooklyn according to the federal census. William was 27 years old and employed as a machinist making envelopes in a paper factory. Anna was 23, Emily was "2 and 10/12" and George was "1 and 5/12."

By this time, William and Anna had somehow scraped up enough money to buy a lot in a rural section of Queens, and William's sister bought the lot next door. Despite having never built a house, William did just that.

This was a remarkable feat because William had no knowledge or experience building a home. But he studied other houses and figured out how to do it step-by-step. The house was built on locust posts and Anna did much of the digging for those posts. Little by little, William built one section of the house at a time, including an outhouse. It's hard to imagine, but he worked in bitter cold weather and hand-carried all the materials on the train and trolley from Brooklyn to Queens. William did not own a car at the time and it was many years before he was able to afford one.

At first the house was pretty primitive. The family used kerosene because gas and electricity were not yet available. My father, who was still a young boy, remembered one time when a kerosene lamp exploded. Everyone ran out of the house and fortunately, William was able to extinguish the flames in time. My father also remembered there was a grate in the floor that you could stand on for warmth from the furnace in the cellar below.

Building the house in Queens

The house was located on top of a hill and you could see straight down to Jamaica Bay. There were woods all around with lots of rabbits and small animals. At local farms close by, my father said you could pick berries and delicious, juicy tomatoes. The area was so rural that after it snowed, there were no visible roads to follow so Anna would pull Emily and George to school on a sleigh. A sandy road ran in front of their house that was not paved until many years later.

Since the roads were dirt, my father said his socks would get all crusty from sweat and sand after he'd been out playing. His mother would then have to scrub clothes in a wash basin – after first boiling the water – and it was very hard work. Remembering his mother washing clothes with a scrub board and with perspiration pouring down her face was an image he could never forget.

The finished house had brick veneer, a garage underneath and a big stoop out front. Eventually, Anna's brother, Fred, installed heat and plumbing and the city dug up the property to install an underground sewer line. Over 90 years later, the house is still standing at 133-44 123rd Street, Ozone Park, Queens.

William worked long hours at his job and Anna worked very hard as well. She was an excellent cook and kept their house immaculate. My father said Thanksgiving dinner was an extra special occasion. Anna would have to pluck the feathers off the turkey and pull out the guts which was a tough job (that I can't even think about)! Right after Thanksgiving, she would start making cookies and by Christmas she had a big tub of them.

At Christmas, I remember my grandmother's Christmas tree standing on a big table in the living room. Underneath was a miniature, old-fashioned village that covered the entire length of the table. It must have taken her days to set up (and put away!) and I found it so fascinating to imagine all the little shoppers and skaters and sleigh-riders enjoying their holiday season. Now, I too, set up a village at Christmas, no doubt influenced by the one she had so many years ago.

Anna enjoyed writing poetry and was quite talented at drawing with pen and ink. She was an excellent seamstress as well. She crocheted beautiful tablecloths and doilies, and sewed all of her daughter's clothes. When I was a child, she made a complete wardrobe for one of my dolls, including an elaborate wedding gown with all the accessories. Anna was very meticulous and a perfectionist in everything she did.

My grandmother and I often talked about animals because she was an extreme animal lover (as was her mother and my father). When my father was young, he said they had a cat and two dogs. One dog stayed outside probably for security. They also had a canary that Anna kept in a cage and covered at night. One morning when she removed the cover she was shocked to discover a mouse in the cage eating the birdseed! My grandmother loved to feed the outside birds too. She had a birdbath made especially for her by a bricklayer. It was probably quite expensive because it had cut glass in the bottom. I remember the birdbath in the front yard and with what care my grandmother cleaned it to make sure the birds had a nice, cool, clean drink of water.

Anna was physically strong. (My father said from digging those post holes for the house). She was feisty and not afraid of anything – except thunder and lightning! During thunderstorms she would wake everyone up and make them play cards. And for some inexplicable reason, she would also put away the silver.

On "Black Thursday," October 24, 1929, the stock market crashed which set off the Great Depression. It was the worst economic downturn seen to date and impacted the daily life of most American families. About a quarter of the U.S. workforce was unemployed, but fortunately, William continued to work. According to the 1930 federal census, William was an "adjuster in a paper factory." The census also indicated that the Eckhardt family owned a radio.

There had never been anything like radio before. It was so new and so exciting! It brought famous people right into your living room and you could hear news the very same day it happened. No doubt, the family gathered round to hear popular comedy programs of the day like *Amos n' Andy*, and *The Jack Benny Show*, as well as soap operas, sporting events and swing music. Money was scarce so the radio set was a welcome and free diversion from the everyday hardships people faced during the Depression.

By the early 1930s, the family finally owned a car and spent summer vacations at Lake Ronkonkoma, Long Island. William and Anna bought a lot there and had a bungalow built with a porch added later. They also had a well dug that went 118' down and provided icy cold water all-year round. William could only go to the Lake on weekends, however, because he worked all week as well as ½ days on Saturdays.

The bungalow was in the woods and my father said there was always plenty of work to be done so he would work ½ a day, painting, pulling out stumps, pouring concrete and digging a pit for the outhouse – before   heading down to the Lake for a swim.

In July, 1937, Anna and Williams' daughter, Emily, was the first to leave the nest. She married a young man from Brooklyn named Arthur Brennen. They settled down in Jamaica, Queens and had two children: Lynne and Tom. Eventually, they moved to Massapequa Park, Long Island.

George married five years after his sister. At Lake Ronkonkoma, he had become friendly with the family who owned and operated Haug's Casino, a food stand with parking and bathing lockers on the Lake. There were three boys and two girls in the Haug family. George was quite the diver (as seen in 35 millimeter home movies) and he must have impressed one of the Haug girls named Marion who was a locker girl. Having known each other for years from summers spent at the Lake, Marion and George fell in love and got engaged in October, 1941.

That same month George was drafted into the Army Air Corps in support of another World War that had erupted in Europe. Understandably, Anna was very distraught and my father said she cried and carried on when her boy, "Sonny," as she called him, left the house to go off to war.

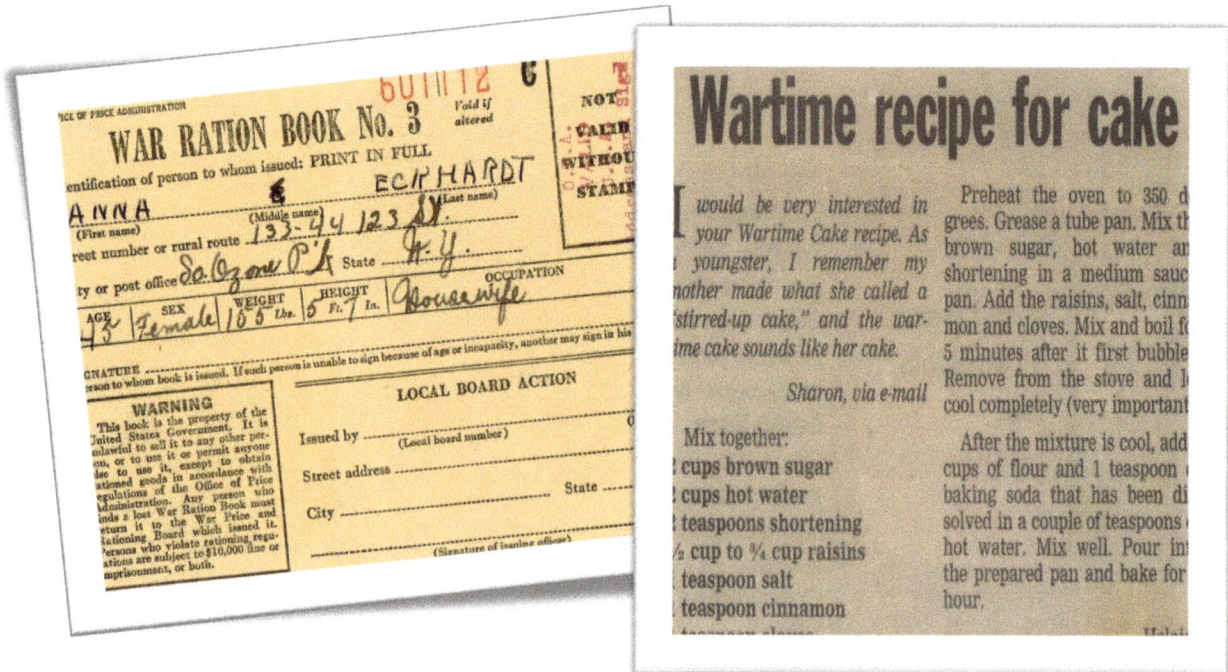

After the Japanese attack on Pearl Harbor and the U.S. entry into the War, everyday life changed for most Americans. Panic gripped the country for fear of another attack – this time on the U.S. mainland and as a result, the majority of Americans understood the need for sacrifice to achieve victory. Limits were set on how much food, gas and clothing could be purchased and families were issued War Ration Books and ration stamps that were necessary to buy everything from meat, sugar, fat, butter, vegetables, fruit, gasoline, tires, clothing, silk, nylon and fuel oil.

During the war, Anna would make my mother a "war cake" for her birthday and she loved it. The ingredients were simple: brown sugar, spices and raisins or nuts. Many years later my mother found the recipe and was thrilled.

Mother and daughter, Anna and Emily

Anna, George and Marion Eckhardt

Dear Marion & George,

Inclosed find a gift for both of you on your Paper Anniversary 1 whole year, don't save it, have a good time & injoy your Anniversary, lets hope everything will be over until the next one rolls by. Lots of luck to you both, from Daddy & I.

Love,

Mom & Pop.

Card to Marion and George for their one-year anniversary, November 1943

William and Anna, Labor Day, 1944

Anna and grandson, *Georgie Eckhardt, 1949*

In the 1950s, William retired and then Anna and William moved again, for the final time. They sold their house in Queens and bought land in Babylon, Long Island, not far from where their daughter, Emily, was living in Massapequa Park. My father designed the house for his parents and then William and Anna had it built. But William did much of the work himself – inside finishing and outside landscaping, as well as the patio – with my father's help. They also sold off several wooded lots over the years.

Life was good. William and Anna had worked very hard for many years and now had chance to enjoy their retirement. William tended to his lawn and garden and kept the house in pristine condition. I can still see him now puffing away on his pipe or cigar as he sat in the shade of his garage contentedly watching the world go by.

Lawrence Welk

Meanwhile, Anna loved to sew and crochet and she was an excellent cook. She enjoyed writing letters to TV personalities like Arthur Godfrey and Lawrence Welk; she also wrote to several Presidents and their wives. Anna was very outgoing and enjoyed spending time with her neighbors. She and William were both popular on the block because all the neighborhood kids knew they could stop by for a chat and an ice cream Popsicle anytime.

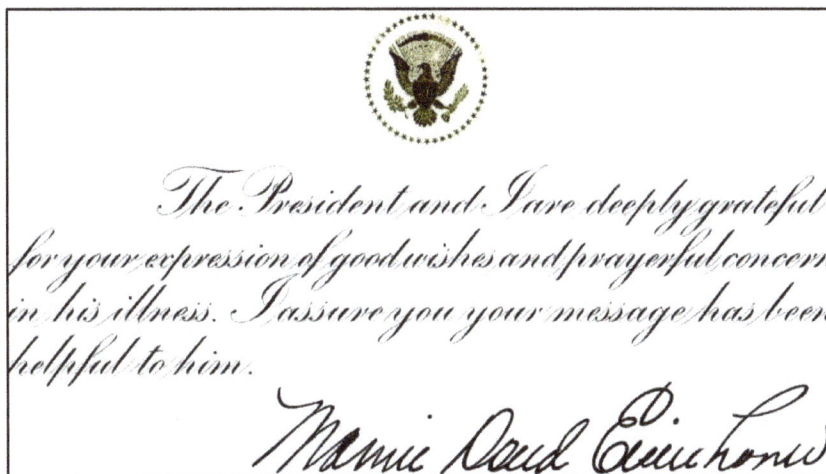

The President and I are deeply grateful for your expression of good wishes and prayerful concern in his illness. I assure you your message has been helpful to him.

Mamie Doud Eisenhower

Anna had had a couple of mild heart attacks. One day she told her husband she wasn't feeling well and she was just going to lie down for a while. When he checked on her, she had passed away peacefully. Anna was 77 years old and was buried on May 10th 1974, in Cypress Hills Cemetery, Brooklyn, in the same plot as her mother and sister. William lived to the age of 96 and is buried beside Anna – they shared their lives together for 59 years.

What I remember most about my grandmother is what a vivacious and fun-loving person she was. My grandparents were kind, hard-working people and they were always very kind to me. I treasure the memories I have of both of them and feel very fortunate that they were such a positive influence in my life.

Anna and William, 50th Anniversary, 1965

Anna and William dancing at Louise Eckhardt and Joan Haug's confirmation party, May 1969

Drawings by Anna Bahn

This one is signed by Anna Bahn

Anna's beautiful black onyx and diamond ring with white gold filigree

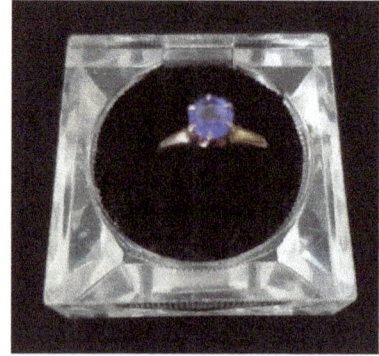

A ring that Anna wore every day

An oak sewing box that belonged to Anna. It says Wheeler & Wilson Sewing Machines on the top.

Ceramic figurines that belonged to Anna. Some are stamped with "Occupied Japan" on the bottom. I think her collection inspired my collection of carved wooden people from different countries.

A towel rack made by William Eckhardt

A gorgeous 3 piece set that belonged to Anna Eckhardt

Edward Henry Haug

The Edward & Louise Haug Family

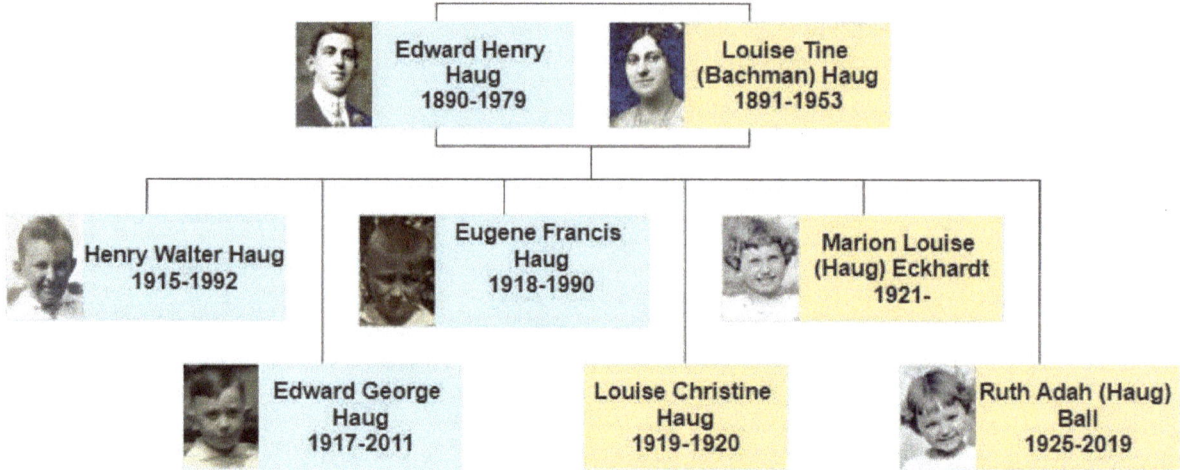

Henry & Edward Haug

Edward Henry
Haug
1890-1979

Louise Tine
(Bachman)
Haug
1891-1953

Henry Walter Haug
1915-1992

Barbara (Jaax)
Haug
1930-2007

Edward George
Haug
1917-2011

Ruth (Newdoll)
Haug
1916-1962

Virginia (Laube)
Reinhardt
Haug
1927-2017

Eugene Haug

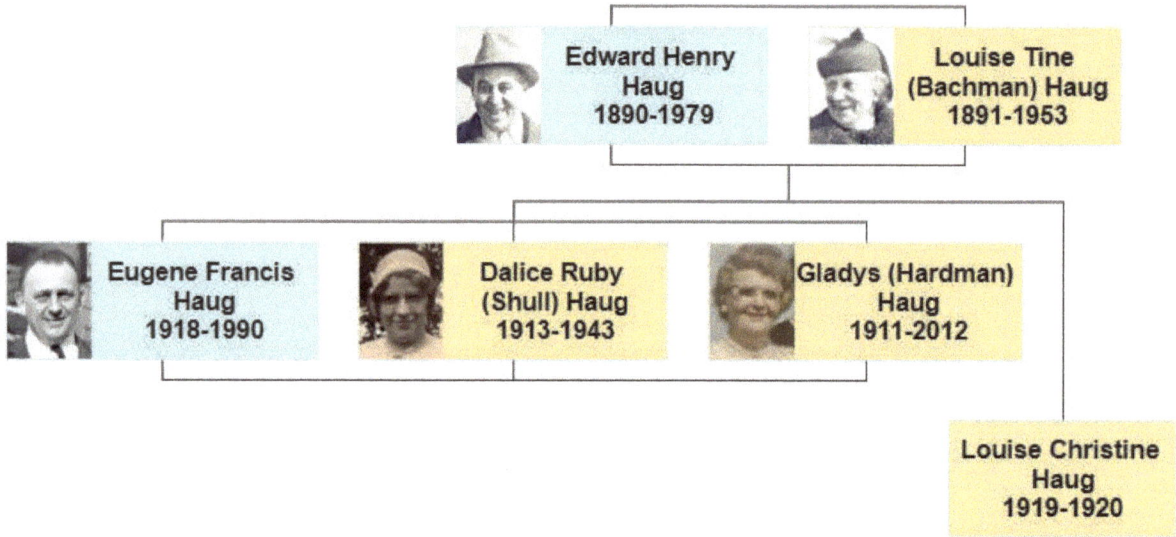

Marion & Ruth Haug

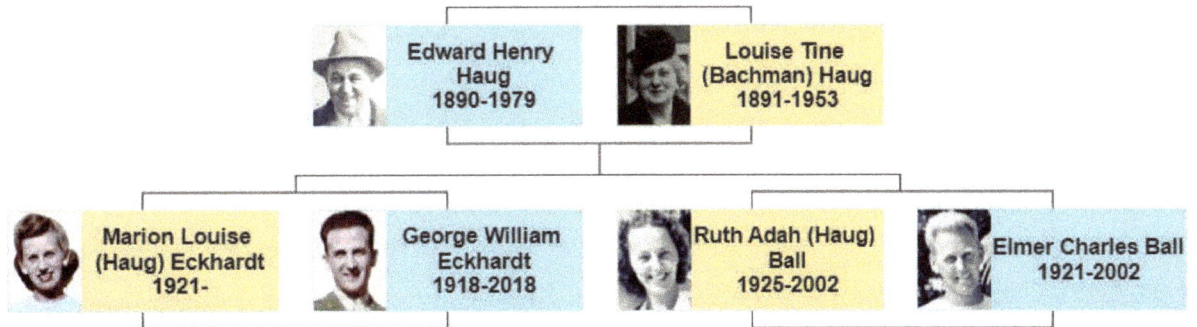

EDWARD HENRY HAUG

"Be true to your teeth or they will be false to you" was just one of the pearls of wisdom espoused by my grandfather!

His name was Edward Henry Haug and he was a very smart businessman, a prominent member in his community and the patriarch of our family. He also had lots of sage advice. For example, one morning when I was a teenager my grandfather called and we were having a nice chat. I had gotten home very late the night before and was in big trouble. I told my grandfather that I was in the doghouse and he said, "Louise, did you have a good time?" I replied, "Oh Grandpa, I had a great time!" And he said, "That's wonderful! Just remember, for every good time you have, you will probably have three times that aren't that great – so when you're having a good time, go ahead and have a really good time!"

His nine grandchildren adored him and fondly remember the "candy line" at every family get-together. My grandfather always brought a big bag of nickel candy and we would go around in a circle, stick our hand in that bag and pull out all sorts of goodies: Turkish Taffy, Licorice, Chuckles, Planters Peanut bars, Sugar Daddy pops, Reeds Life Savers, etc. We collected quite a hoard and then we would go off and trade amongst ourselves.

My grandfather was a very kind and generous person to a wide circle of family and friends. He was a fantastic businessman and a leader in his community. But nothing was more important to him than Family. And when I was growing up, we had many family get-togethers throughout the year that rotated between his house in Brooklyn, my parent's house in Staten Island and the rest of my aunts and uncles in Queens and Long Island.

But hands down, our very favorite get-together was going to Coney Island every summer! This was a really big deal, on par with Christmas in my mind! We went on rides all day long paid for by my grandfather and then he treated us all to dinner in a nice restaurant afterwards. This was a day not to be missed (even if you had the measles, which I did one year, but we went anyway)! Christmas at my grandfather's house was also a wonderful day with a big meal, lots of presents, home movies and a real live Santa – one of our uncles or great-uncles dressed up with the white beard and red Santa suit.

Born March 24, 1890, in Brooklyn, New York, Edward Henry Haug was one of five children. He had two older sisters, Eva and Henrietta, and a younger brother and sister, Walter and Marguerite. The family lived at 1850 Fulton St. above a small variety store run by Edward's mother, Henrietta. She sold candy, tobacco, school supplies, toys, and buns and rolls – even ice cream in the summer – at a time when ice cream could only be bought in the winter. She worked hard and long hours, opening at 6:00 AM and not closing till 11:00 P.M. When they were old enough, the girls helped out in the store too and sold candy to the children customers.

1892 - Ed Haug with baby brother Walter

Henry Haug, Edward's father, started his own express business in 1882. With his one horse and one wagon, he hauled merchandise around New York City. In time business picked up and he was able to expand with more horses, wagons and additional help.

His sons, Edward and Walter, were kept busy helping their father after school. They took care of the bedding for the horses and paid the feed bill and the horse shoer every week. Eddie was affectionately called "horseshit Eddie" by his classmates because he always had to clean out the horses' stalls before he arrived at school. Eddie and Walter were so busy that the rest of the family never saw them except at mealtimes.

Fulton St. in Bedford Stuyvesant, Brooklyn, was an exciting place to grow up in the late 19th century. It was a main thoroughfare and a thriving business area with theaters and many stores. The street had a lot of traffic and noise, especially with the Elevated train running overhead right in front of their store and residence as depicted in this 1905 postcard.

FULTON STREET and ELEVATED R. R., BROOKLYN, N. Y

The Haug family rented the building at 1850 Fulton St. The store was in the front and behind the store was the kitchen. This is where the family would often play records on one of those early cabinet phonographs with a big horn. Upstairs were three bedrooms and a parlor heated by an oil heater and later by gas and eventually electric. In later years, the family also acquired a square piano.

Eddie and his four siblings attended Public School 70 about five blocks away on Patchen Ave. Going to and from school, they walked past their father's stable on Patchen Ave. and their grandparent's grocery store on the corner of Patchen Ave. and Chauncey Street. On his way home, Eddie would stop and deliver grocery orders for his grandfather.

Church was an important part of growing up in the Haug household. Both of Eddie's parents had belonged to the same church since the early 1870s, the Brooklyn Reformed Church on Herkimer St. Eddie was baptized and confirmed in this church as well. Every Sunday, Eddie and his brothers and sisters walked about a mile to attend Sunday school and each contributed two cents for the offering. They

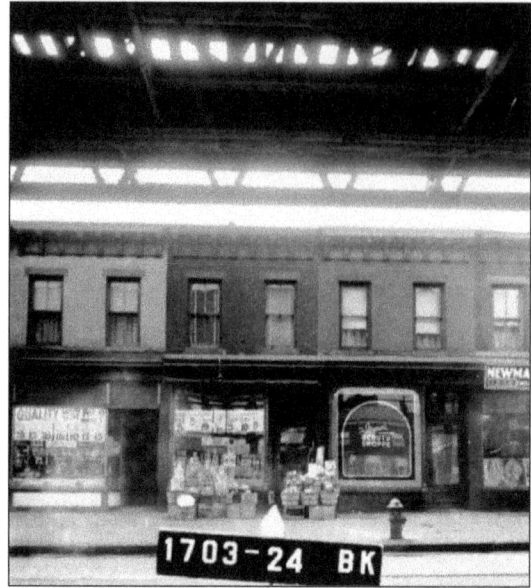

1850 Fulton St. Photo taken by the WPA in th1940s

were all active in church and participated in various activities: the choir, young people's society, Boy's Brigade and best of all, the annual Anniversary Day parades.

Unique to Brooklyn, Anniversary Day was a long-standing tradition and a public school holiday. It was always held the first Thursday in June to celebrate the founding of the first Sunday school in Brooklyn. Wearing their Sunday best, boys and girls from all over the borough's schools would march behind military bands with banners and tassels. As reported in *The Brooklyn Daily Eagle*, June 6, 1902, "From their widely separated homes in the big borough, these boys and girls of the Sunday schools gathered at 20 different points and paraded the streets in the happy and frolicsome manner that befits youth." No doubt, Eddie, who was 12 years old at the time, was one of the 90,000 children that marched that day.

A few years later, he was mentioned in *The Brooklyn Daily Eagle*, December 14, 1908, when a Ladies organization of the German Reformed Church presented a flag to the Boy's Brigade during an elaborate ceremony. "The congregation was large and augmented by many veterans of the Civil War. In addition, there were 50 uniformed boys of the Boy's Brigade in attendance under the captaincy of Edward Haug."

In 1906 when Eddie was a teenager, the Haug family attended a very important social event. The eldest daughter of their Uncle Joseph Bermel, (who was borough President of Queens), was getting married. It was a very elaborate affair and as reported in the *Brooklyn Times Union*, about 300 people attended and a catered wedding breakfast was served afterward "in the parlor of the Bermel homestead on Metropolitan Avenue." The three Haug sisters bought new dresses for the occasion and their father hired a closed funeral coach, as this was the only way to transport the family there. It was a wonderful affair (according to Eddie's sister Eva). The Haug family even had a professional photo taken to commemorate the occasion.

Edward Haug's Confirmation – 1905

Ed outside the Brooklyn Reformed Church

1906 - Haug family attended the Bermel wedding. Top Row: Henrietta, Edward, Walter, Eva. Bottom Row: Henry, Marguerite, Henrietta

Eddie attended school until the 8th grade. When he graduated, he went to work driving a horse and wagon for the baker who supplied his mother with rolls and buns every morning for her store. He had to get up at 2:00 AM so he rented a room nearby for $2.00 per week. However, he did not do this for long. Around 1908, Eddie's father had an opportunity to buy out the business of another expressman, a Mr. Seiler. Now his father owned four horses and two extra wagons so it made more sense for Eddie to quit working for the baker and work for his father full time.

Around this same time, Eddie's mother gave up her store and the family was able to move to a larger home. Henry and Henrietta bought a 2 ½ story house in the same Bedford Stuyvesant neighborhood, at 119 Marion St. Now, they no longer had to hear the elevated trains rattling along the tracks but it was so quiet they couldn't sleep. Conveniently, the back of this house adjoined the driveway of Henry's stable on Patchen Ave. On this 1908 Sanborn map, you can see Ed's grandfather's grocery store at the corner of Chauncey Street and Patchen Avenue. Behind the store is the stable represented by an X."

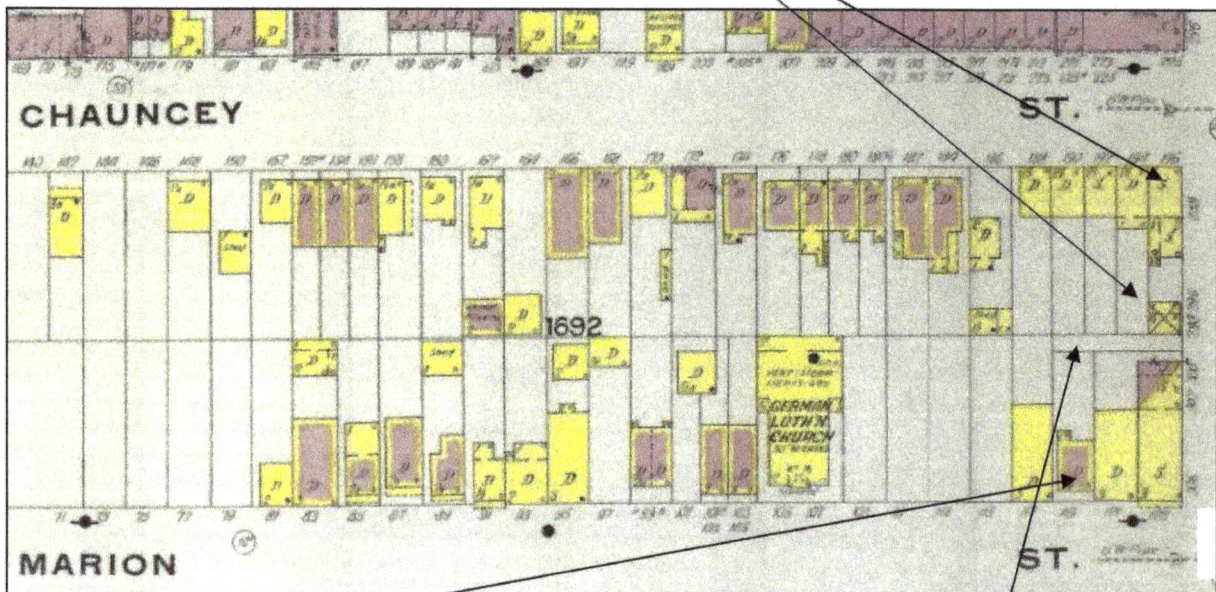

Here is the home at 119 Marion St. and the driveway behind it that connected to the stable. (On this map, "D" stands for dwelling and "S" stands for store. Yellow represents a frame building and pink/yellow represents a frame building that is brick lined).

In February 1910, tragedy struck the Haug family. Eddie's father, Henry, was admitted to the German Hospital of Brooklyn. Although the doctor assured the family that Henry would do well, he died of acute pneumonia and nephritis six days after his operation. He was only 49 years old. Just the year before, Henry and Henrietta had celebrated their 25th anniversary with a second marriage ceremony at the German Reformed Church and a large banquet afterward with about 50 guests.

Eddie was 19 years old at the time of his father's death. His brother, Walter, was 17 and their mother felt she had no choice but to take Walter out of school to help Eddie run the express business. Fortunately, the two boys were very familiar with the business and their employees stayed with them. Their Uncle Charlie, (Henrietta's brother) visited all the firms they dealt with and offered bond for the boys. Fortunately, the firms had confidence in the brothers and continued to hire Haug's Express to haul freight around New York City. It was a family business and everyone pitched in to help: their mother, Henrietta, took orders, their sister, Henrietta, did all the bookkeeping and everyone took turns answering the phone. The boys worked very hard and the business did well under the boys' management.

When Marguerite, the youngest sibling, turned 21 (April 26, 1917), Henrietta settled her husband's estate. In a legal Bill of Sale, she sold the express and delivery business to her two sons for one dollar. The three daughters, Eva, Henrietta and Marguerite, agreed to the sale and each signed the document. Officially, Haug's Express was incorporated in March 1920, and listed under, "New Incorporations" in the *New York Times*. Edward and Walter both owned 49 shares of the company and their wives, Louise and Hattie, owned one share each.

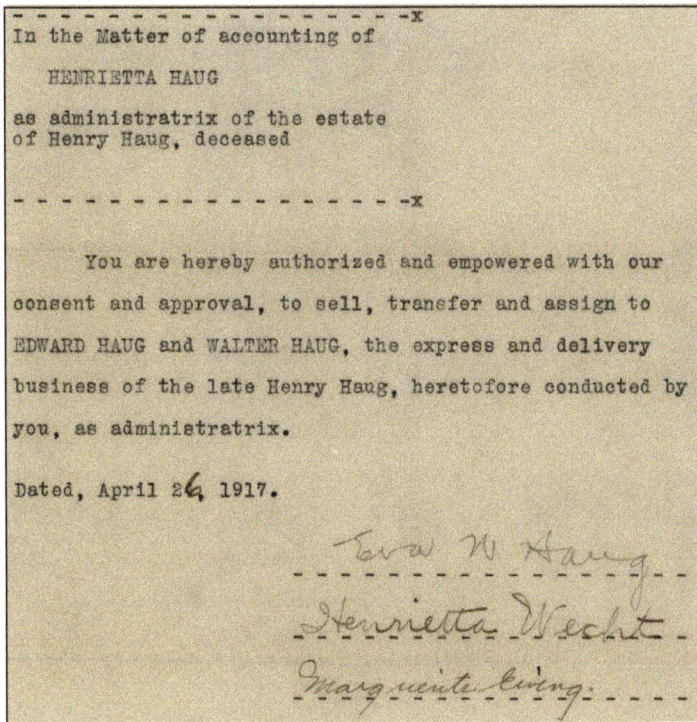

Original Bill of sale for Haug's Express with the signatures of Ed's 3 sisters: Eva Haug, Henrietta Wecht and Marguerite Ewing

In a 1910 postcard of Haug's Express, Ed is in the center between two horses and Walter is standing and holding a horse. There are four wagons in the photo, three with open sides and one with slats – but all had canvas curtains on the roof to let down in the rain. At that time all the drivers wore a shirt and tie while on the wagons. The house behind the wagons was 119 Marion St. and the stable entrance was around the corner on Patchen Ave.

Haug's Express also had an office at 85 Reade St. in lower Manhattan. The horses worked so hard and sometimes it was bitterly cold driving the horse and wagon – especially going across the Brooklyn Bridge into Manhattan. The horses knew the route and while the driver was unloading a shipment at one store, the horses would walk down to the next store. On occasion, Ed would fall asleep on the way home but the horses always knew the way.

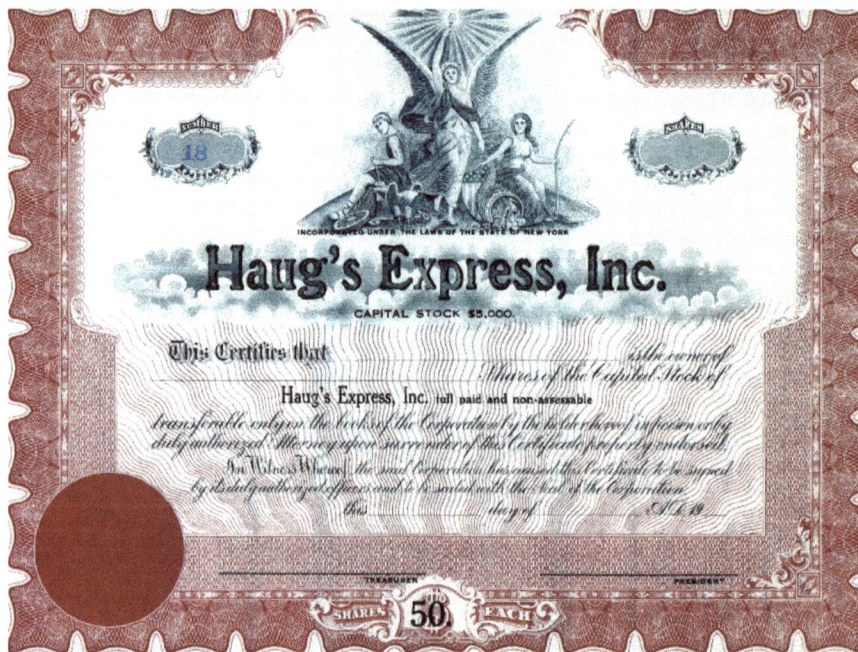

A couple years later Ed met a young lady, Louise Bachman, who was living in Queens. She worked as a forelady at a company in downtown Manhattan where Ed stopped every day to pick up shipments. He began courting "Weezie" as he affectionately called her and one of his letters survives from March 7, 1912:

Dear Louise,

I thought I would drop you a few lines, being I cannot get out to see you, although I would like too (*sic*). I tried my best to get over to your house tonight, but did not get home until 9 o'clock and by the time I would get over to your house all the folks would be to bed, and then I would have to come home disappointed.

I mist (*sic*) you Tuesday evening and was in warren street until 5:30 and had a bottle of oil of camfore (*sic*)which I was going to give you for your throat, which cured me the second night, that is between the cough drops, cold water and oil of camfore, (*sic*) but did not see you. I then thought you were sick for I saw all the rest of the crew except the one I cared to see.

Yesterday I met Reich in the hall and he said to me <u>No Brooklyn</u> so I walked out. Today he had a package, but did not say anything about the forelady not being their (*sic*) in fact he was to (*sic*) busy or worried to tell me his trubles (*sic*).

The folks are all out except the two ~~muts~~ dogs and their (*sic*) never out except for an airing, and to make good use of my time I thought I would write you. Walter told me you were sick and could not go to the Tea Party, but that is all he said. I will find out the rest of the news when they get home, and I will make it my business to stay up until they get home too.

If you are still sick by Saturday don't come over here or even try to. I will come to your house even if I do come late, but I hope it won't be that long.

Will close now my eyes are getting the best of me and further more I have to get this letter in the mail box before 10:30, if I don't you may not get it until next week. You know we get such fine service over here. Best wishes to all from all.

Yours Forever,

Eddie

Excuse all mistakes

Louise Bachman and Ed Haug announced their engagement at a party in December, 1912 and they were married on October 19, 1913, in a Catholic church, St. Brigid's Rectory in Brooklyn. Walter and Louise's sister, Mary Bachman, were the witnesses. For their honeymoon, the couple traveled to Baltimore and stayed at the home of Ed's Aunt Lena Fink. Upon their return, Ed and Louise took up residence right next door to Ed's mother, at 117 Marion Street, where their first child, Henry, was born on January 6, 1915.

Following family tradition, baby Henry was baptized at the German Reformed Church. But Louise's sister, Mamie, did not approve of this Protestant ceremony and scooped up baby Henry to have him baptized properly at a Catholic church.

Ed usually worked late so Louise and little Henry spent a lot of time next door with Ed's mother and sisters. Louise's mother-in-law taught her how to crochet and eventually Louise crocheted a bedspread for every bed in the house.

Ed was the first of his siblings to marry. In April 1915, his sister Henrietta married Frank Wecht in an elaborate affair held at the Bedford Mansion in Brooklyn. The following year in a double ceremony Ed's brother, Walter, married Hattie Reinhardt, and his sister, Marguerite, married George Ewing at the German Reformed Church. Ed did the honor of escorting both of his sisters, Henrietta and Marguerite, down the aisle. The last of the five Haug siblings, Eva, married Edwin Lenning in 1918 during World War I.

War had been raging in Europe since 1914. Initially, the United States had a policy of neutrality and President Wilson won election in 1916 with the slogan, "He kept us out of the war." However, public opinion started to shift after the sinking of the British ocean liner, the Lusitania, by a German U-boat. Over 2,000 people perished in that disaster including 128 Americans. The Germans had also attempted to coopt the Mexican government into an alliance against the U.S. Both of these events propelled President Wilson to request Congress to act. The United States declared war against Germany in April, 1917.

President Wilson had intended to support the war effort with an all-volunteer force but too few men were signing up. Therefore, in April, 1917, Congress passed the Selective Service Act which authorized the federal government to raise a national army by conscription.

There were three registrations. The first, on June 5, 1917, was for all men between the ages of 21 and 30. Ed signed up on that day. His registration card stated that he was an expressman, in business for himself and employed at 720 Herkimer St. He was living at 119 Marion St. and he had a wife and two children. He also claimed an exemption for a "rupture" (and it is known that he wore a truss, probably for a hernia). Fortunately, Ed did not have to serve. He was exempt because he was probably categorized as Class IV, "a married registrant with a dependent

spouse and dependent children with insufficient family income if drafted." Ed's brother, Walter, also signed up on June 5, 1917. He was an expressman living and working at 720 Herkimer St. He claimed an exemption because he was married and expecting a child in 2 weeks.

Another fear gripped the country in 1918 – the outbreak of a deadly influenza virus. The conditions of World War I – overcrowding at Army training camps and overseas troop movements – helped spread the disease in the United States. This pandemic was the deadliest in the 20th century and lasted 2 years. It ultimately infected about 500 million people and killed at least 50 million worldwide and 675,000 in the United States.

This is the backdrop against which Louise and Eddie started their young family. By the war's end, the couple had three little boys: Henry born in 1915, Edward in 1917 and Eugene in 1918. Then they had three girls: Louise in

Louise with Eugene, born August 17, 1918 and Edward, born January 12, 1917

1919, Marion in 1921 and Ruth in 1924. All of the children were born in a hospital and not at home, which was unusual for the time. But sadly, baby Louise was not well. On the advice of doctors, her parents took her to the seashore to convalesce but she passed away on the train ride home. Little Louise had been ill for 3 months and she was only 6 months old when she died of bronco-pneumonia. The funeral was held at the family home and one can only imagine the sadness of her grieving parents.

Louise with Marion, born August 16, 1921 and Ruth, born Jan. 8, 1925

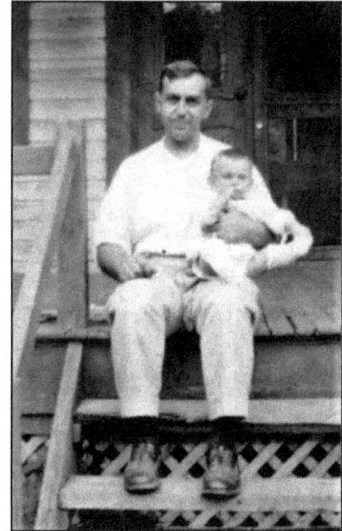

1925 - Edward with baby Ruth

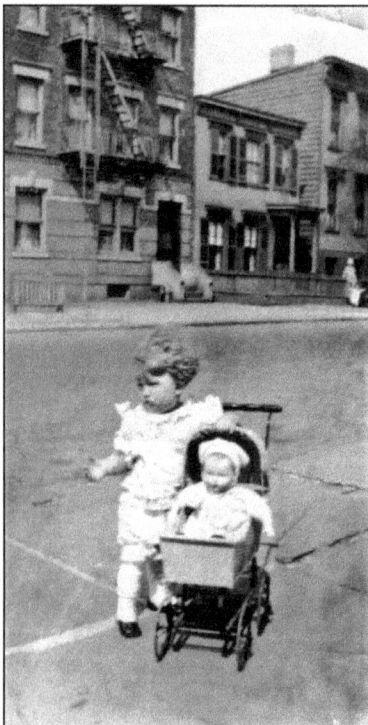

Marion outside 119 Marion St. She was named after the street she was born on.

By 1920, the federal census shows that Louise and Ed and their four young children were living at 119 Marion St. and they were now the owners of the home. Henrietta, (Ed's mother) had previously owned the house and she had added a floor above as well as a square stoop. Henrietta was renting an upstairs apartment in that house, as was Ed's sister, Marguerite, and her family.

Walter had purchased a house nearby at 720 Herkimer St. and both he and Ed operated Haug's Express from this address. Living upstairs, was their sister, Eva, and her husband Ted. A couple years later, Eddie bought the house next to Walter's

119 Marion St. - WPA photo from the 1940s

at 718 Herkimer St. so the brothers were living side-by-side. Upstairs at 718 Herkimer was Louise's sister, Mamie, who enjoyed looking out the window to watch all the activity below. She was a large woman and when she died, she had to be hoisted out of the house by piano movers.

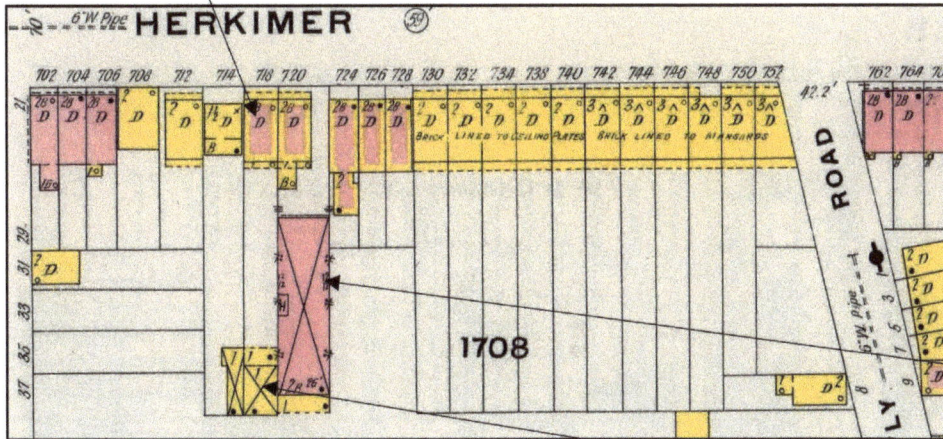

1908 Sanborn map – 718 & 720 Herkimer St.   2B= a 2-story story building with basement
D=dwelling. Yellow=frame building. Pink=brick. Pink/yellow=frame building, brick lined. X=stable.

For many years, the previous owner of 720 Herkimer St. (Al Culliford) had had a livery business there with dozens of horses. The property had a large basement and a big two-story stable in back, which could be used as a garage to store wagons or vehicles. Behind 718 Herkimer St. was another smaller garage (previously a stable) that could store about four vehicles – so it was an ideal location for the brothers' expanding business.

The garage behind 720 Herkimer St. had an office on one side that was heated with a big pot belly stove. Above the garage was a large loft where the wagons were stored and a huge lift to elevate the wagons up to the second floor. Underneath the two houses was an extensive basement that had stalls for as many as 40 horses.

720 Herkimer St. (WPA photo from the 1940s).

718 Herkimer St. (WPA photo from the 1940s)

My mother told me that way in the back of that basement were rooms and her father let her use one as an "office" when she was a kid. There her friends, Helen Delafield and Jean Van Winkle, would draw and color. She also remembers there was a huge furnace down there that heated the two houses and the apartments above. My cousin, Joan, and I remember going down to that basement once but we were very young. It was dark and scary and there seemed to be room after room after room. In the 1960s, my grandfather set up a fall-out shelter in that basement with canned goods, flashlights, etc. You could go underground from the basement to the garage without going outside.

By 1917, Edward and Walter started converting their express business from horses to trucks. Their first truck was made by The Autocar Company and it had hard tires (not air) on the back of the truck and rear brakes. The August 1920 publication of *Autocar Messenger,* mentioned Haug's Express, Inc. of Brooklyn, NY, as having placed a recent order and they were listed as a repeat customer as well. The Haug brothers also purchased an early Ford truck but it was described as "troublesome." This entry in *The Evening Telegram*, (September 26, 1919), under "Automobiles for Sale" might be referring to that very truck:

"COMMERCIAL ton Ford, 1917 in good condition, $350. HAUG'S EXPRESS. 720 Herkimer St."

The purchase of the first personal car in the family was a big event! Ed's sister, Eva, bought a 1917 Model-T Ford touring car for $381, including $8.00 for the speedometer, $1.50 for the tire holder and $20.00 for the demountable rims. It had four cylinders and a two-speed transmission that made it easy to drive. And its high chassis was designed to clear the bumps in rural roads. What an adventure it must have been to drive an automobile at this time! Edward and Walter each took a day off from work to take their young families, along with their mother, to the beach.

The 1920s marked the beginning of the automobile era – a symbol of freedom – for now people could go anywhere anytime, if muddy, bumpy roads allowed. Car trips took longer though and inevitably, one of the Haug children would have to go to the bathroom en route. So Edward came up with a unique solution. He drilled a hole in the floor and added a funnel and a seat on top so a child could urinate directly into the street. One time a fellow traveler passed Edward and told him his car was leaking. He thanked him kindly and they went on their way.

Ed installed another modification in his car too – a jump seat (originally from a taxi) for the two girls to sit facing their brothers. But looking backwards made Ruth carsick. And when the girls stood up, the seat would also pop up and pitch them forward. Of course there was always a lot of bickering among the five kids and their mom would turn around and swat anyone within arm's reach when they misbehaved.

Thanksgiving was always a big road trip for the family. They celebrated at Selina's house (Louise's sister) in Philadelphia. It was a strange house with a small bathroom in the kitchen that had just a curtain and no door. And upstairs there was a room with a tub that you had to walk through to get to a bedroom. My mother remembers that her family would stay overnight and all five kids would sleep sideways in one bed.

Edward and Louise also took trips to Martinsville, NJ for Easter. There they stayed at the Hoffman Farm and were joined by Walter's family too. All the cousins must have had a grand time together. My mother, Marion, was very young but she does remember walking in the mountains and lots of small animals there.

Lake Ronkonkoma

Lake Ronkonkoma on Long Island, NY, had a profound and lasting impact on the Haug family for decades. During the late 19th and early 20th century, Lake Ronkonkoma was an exclusive summer resort for the wealthy and famous from New York City. William Vanderbilt had constructed a home there in 1910 which attracted well-to-do families who used the area for their summer homes. By the 1920s the automobile brought dramatic change to the area. Roads began to appear everywhere and gasoline pumps were installed in and around town. And with the extension of the Long Island Motor Parkway (also known as the Vanderbilt Parkway) to Lake Ronkonkoma, motorists could now drive all the way from New York City without stopping – for this was the first roadway designed for automobile use only (no horses) and the first to use overpasses and bridges to eliminate intersections. The Lake became more accessible for more people – and they could enjoy what this beautiful lake had to offer – boating, bathing, sailing and fishing. Many beaches and pavilions sprang up around the lake with waterwheels, floats and slides, and music and dancing. And on Sundays, a big attraction was a man named Jimmy Horning, a daredevil who used to parachute into the lake from a small plane.

In the summer of 1924, Ed, Louise and their five children visited the white, sandy shores of Lake Ronkonkoma. They stayed at the famed Lake Front Hotel and must have had a wonderful time for they returned the next summer. On the hotel property, in addition to the carriage house and stables, was a large vacant house with six bedrooms called "The Casino." It was described in a brochure as having two stories: a "place for reading, writing, sewing, conversation, dancing or other social purposes on the first floor" and a billiard room on the second floor. The "whole building is surrounded by a broad piazza every part of which is reached by the cool and balmy breezes which constantly play around it thus affording sheltering and refreshing nooks of ease and comfort on even the warmest days." The Haug family rented the Casino in 1925 with an option to buy.

The following year Ed and Louise purchased the Casino for $9,000. It was on the lakefront and the white sandy beach was right across the road. However, bathers were not allowed access to the beach or the water unless they owned the land beneath the lake. A man in a rowboat even circled the lake and chased away trespassers. So Ed purchased a parcel of land for $1800 that extended 250' underneath the lake. He also had a small refreshment stand built across the road from their home. Then he purchased bathhouses from Olympia Pavilion and had them floated over to his property – and the Haug family was in business! They called it "Haug's Casino" and it was definitely

a family affair. The five children all had jobs: Henry parked cars for 50 cents each, Edward and Gene ran the refreshment stand and Marion and Ruth were the locker girls in charge of the bathhouse. Regular customers could buy a season locker for $5.00. Marion also made some money when she was a kid by rowing people around the lake.

At the Haug's roadside stand they sold candy and soda at first. Once they installed a stove with a griddle, they added hamburgers, hot dogs and chowder to the menu and they eventually had kegs of beer too. Sometimes Louise would come down to the stand and help out. But Ed only went to the Lake on weekends because he was still running Haug's Express with his brother in Brooklyn. When he was at the Lake, however, Ed enjoyed playing pool, drinking beer and playing cards with his buddies. Louise was the enforcer; she would chase the kids home if they got too noisy or she would have Ed close up the stand if it got too late.

Every time it rained my mother said she and her siblings had to eat up all the hot dogs at the stand. To this day, Marion said,

she doesn't like hot dogs very much. Her father's advice was to never invest in a seasonal business.

Ed's son, Edward, remembered that sometimes en route to Lake Ronkonkoma his father would buy clams from someone selling them on the side of the road, 100 clams for one dollar. He might also stop by an orchard in Port Jefferson, buy bushel baskets of peaches and bring them to the Lake as well.

From left to right: Gene, Marion, Edward and Henry with their parents

Ed and Louise were a very social couple and they hosted many get-togethers at the Lake for family and friends. Here are just a few examples from local newspapers:

Haug children: Henry (tallest), Edward (middle), Gene, Marion (front) and Ruth (youngest)

Sunday, June 12, 1932, *Brooklyn Times Union* – The annual outing of the Ocean Hill Square Club, which brings together the members and their families for a day at the seashore of one of Long Island's pleasure places, will find the craftsmen en route to Lake Ronkonkoma next Sunday morning. The party will go in the private cars of the members leaving the headquarters, Buffalo Hall, Fulton St. and Buffalo Ave., at 9:30 o'clock. The cars will be decorated in bunting, American flags and club insignia. The destination of the outing is Edward Haug's Casino on Main St. in Ronkonkoma. The day will be given over to athletic activities and games and there will be a series of events for the children of the members as well as the grown-ups.

Sunday, July 24, 1932, *Brooklyn Times Union* – Down at Lake Ronkonkoma last Sunday we found a number of prominent craftsmen who were visiting Edward Haug at his pavilion on the lake. A few were from the Ocean Hill Square Club. Some were making merry in the cool waters of the lake, while others indulged in pinochle under the shade of huge beach umbrellas.

August 23, 1932, *Brooklyn Times Union* – With civic problems laid aside for the summer, the Clarence C. Curth Civic Association is devoting itself to social functions. The second outing of the season was reported to have been a success. More than 250 went to Haug's Casino, Lake Ronkonkoma, L.I. Swimming, racing and other sports featured. Prizes were given to the winners of races and games. In buses and private cars the party left 47 Marion St. at 9A.M. and returned about midnight.

Sunday, June 18, 1933, *Brooklyn Times Union* – The members of the Ocean Hill Square Club are making their annual pilgrimage to Lake Ronkonkoma today. More than 50 private automobiles have been registered with the committee to join the caravan. The destination of the party is Edward Haug's Pavilion on the Lake, where boating and bathing will form principal attractions. In the afternoon there will be a baseball game between the married and the single men of the club. There will also be games for the women of the party.

Sunday, July 14, 1935, *Brooklyn Times Union* – The annual bus ride and outing of the Ocean Hill Square Club took place Sunday, June 30, to Haug's Casino, Lake Ronkonkoma. A splendid program of sports and games was arranged by the entertainment committee. The baseball game was won by the Cro-Cean clubs and bunco prizes were also awarded.

Lake Ronkonkoma was a summer hotspot for all ages. And it was a popular place in the winter as well when people enjoyed boating and ice skating on the frozen lake. The Haugs entertained family and friends all-year-round. It was a busy household and everyone was welcome.

People skate and boat on a frozen Lake Ronkonkoma around 1930 (Newsday photo)

By the late 1920s, Ed's mother also lived at Lake Ronkonkoma. After 13 years as a widow, she married a German man named Charles Koenig in June 1923. He was a bachelor and an insurance agent. Henrietta gave up her house on Marion Street in Brooklyn and she and her new husband moved to the Lake where they enjoyed family gatherings with the extended Haug clan.

1928 - Henry, Edward and Gene Haug (in front) skating at the Lake

My father, George Eckhardt, also spent summers at Lake Ronkonkoma. His family had a bungalow there and for $5.00 he could buy a season ticket to swim at Haug's Casino. That's how he became fast friends with all five of the Haug kids.

One time he and Gene Haug drove Grandpa Koenig's Ford down the steps in front of the Haug's house at the Lake. He has no idea why that seemed like a good idea at the time! And when George was younger, he said Ed Haug (his future father-in-law) asked him if he wanted to finish painting the back porch floor of the house. George was thrilled when Ed paid him $2.50 although my father did wonder why he hadn't asked one of his three sons to do the job.

In February, 1938, Gene Haug and George Eckhardt made the local newspaper when they rescued two boys who had fallen into the icy waters of the lake. But the very next day they too had to be rescued when the ice gave way while they were skating. George was able to grab some wood and pull himself out while people standing nearby rescued Gene with the aid of a rope. George ran all the way to the Haug house to try and warm up. Gene, who had been in the water longer, was driven home by car. George said Gene was shivering so much that the whole bed was shaking.

Herkimer Street

Back in Brooklyn, life was always hectic in the Haug household. Louise was the main disciplinarian who kept the five kids in line. She had to since Ed worked late and long hours. She was the boss and one of her hard and fast rules was that everyone had to be home by 6:00 sharp to eat supper. Louise always kept her house neat and tidy. Her daughter Ruth said that you could not leave anything laying around or it would get thrown out.

For Sunday dinners, Louise usually cooked a big roast with potatoes. And for supper the family would have leftover roast, fried potatoes and lots of company. Aunts, uncles and friends often dropped by for there was always plenty of food. Louise made her own noodles and added them to soup. And her sauerbraten with potato balls and bread pudding was everyone's favorite.

On Saturdays, the kids loved to go to the movies. And Henry, as the oldest, was in charge and held on to the money for all of them. My mother said Henry was a cut-up and especially loved to tease his two younger sisters. She said most of the movies were about cowboys and Indians and during the action scenes they were all quiet and attentive. But during the love scenes they talked and fidgeted. Then they galloped all the way home pretending to be cowboys and Indians on horseback.

Each child had chores and each received an allowance. Edward had to get the coffee started in the morning and took a bucket to go get milk and rolls. He also unloaded the trucks and went along on deliveries. Marion had to iron the families' handkerchiefs – at least 50 per week because the boys took one every day. And she said Henry used many of them. The youngest child, Ruth, dried the dishes.

The Haug family was surrounded by relatives and the children had lots of cousins to pal around with. According to the 1930 census, 19 people lived in the two households on Herkimer Street. Besides Ed, Louise and their five children at 718 Herkimer Street, Mamie Schroeder (Louise's sister), her husband Henry, and their two daughters rented an apartment upstairs for $35.00 per month. Next door lived Walter Haug, his wife Hattie, their two daughters and one son, as well as Hattie's brother, George Rheinhardt. Upstairs, Eva Lenning, (Ed's sister), and her husband, Ted, rented an apartment for $38.00 per month.

The 1930 census stated that Ed and Walter Haug owned their homes that were valued at $2,500 each. They were both listed as proprietors of the express company and George Rheinhardt and Ted Lenning were drivers at the company. Three of the four families living at 718 and 720 Herkimer St. owned the latest technology - radio sets.

ELECT

For Alderman

48th Aldermanic Dist.   5th Assembly Dist.

EDWARD

HAUG

Vote B Line No. 10

The 1930s were a difficult time as the Great Depression drastically impacted just about every household. Ed and Walter helped support a number of families – like Mamie living upstairs and Louise's other sister, Selina, in Philadelphia. My mother remembers they donated clothes to other families and friends too.

Politics

In 1935, the Kings County Republican organization nominated Ed to run for political office as the Republican Alderman for the 48th District – the same district he'd lived in his entire life. Not only was Ed a well-known businessman but he had also been a very active member of his community in local civic, fraternal and charitable organizations. He'd been a member of the Kings County Republican Club for 16 years, a Republican Captain for 9 years (of the 7th Enumeration District, 5th Assembly District) – as well as a long-time member of the Anglo Saxon Lodge, the Long Island

Grotto and the Ocean Hill Square Club. Ed was quoted as saying in the *Brooklyn Times Union* that "he enjoys campaigning because he has always been used to long hours in his business."

After Ed won the Primary election in September, "The Friends of the Ed Haug for Alderman Committee" rented a store at 160 Ralph Ave. for $17.00. Then the appointed chairman, treasurer, recording secretary and correspondence secretary went to work to garner support for the November 5th election. Towards the end of the campaign, the Chairman signed a letter that said:

> " . . . We are now entering the last stage of our campaign. We are very anxious to have all present, just for a little heart to heart talk and to give and take advice as to the best course to pursue in electing our good friend Ed.
>
> On Saturday, Nov 2, 1935, we will have an auto parade with red lights, music, horns, etc. and we are very desirous of having you with us whether you have an auto or not. If you have an auto and will favor us with your participation . . . we will see that you are properly equipped with streamers, horns, red lights, etc."

The committee also included five additional sub-committee chairmen to address speakers, voters, finance, press and legal issues. With contributions totaling $358 the Ed Haug for Alderman Committee had funds to pay the rent and other expenses: stationary, cigars, banners, buttons, ribbons, placards, etc. About 35 people contributed to Ed's campaign, mostly in $5 and $10 increments. The biggest contributors were Ed's brother and sisters, Walter ($25), Henrietta ($25) and Eva ($50). Even Ed's two oldest sons, Henry and Edward, contributed $5 each.

On Election day 6,861 people voted for Ed Haug but he lost to John Cashmore who garnered 11,903 votes. Louise was relieved for she hated politics and the fact that her husband was running. A few years later when there was a kidnapping attempt on one of Cashmore's children, Louise was even more relieved that Ed had lost. John Cashmore was later elected Borough President of Brooklyn and a granite marker was erected in front of City Hall to commemorate him. My mother said her father would sometimes sit in the

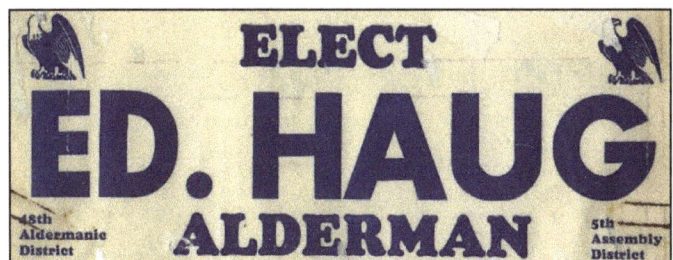

park and look at that historical marker. Perhaps he was reminiscing and wondering what might have been.

Nevertheless, Ed continued his civic activities. On January 1, 1938, he was installed as President of the Ocean Hill Square club by his life-long friend, Benjamin Grinrod. This Masonic club, organized by Grinrod in 1920, had several hundred members and Ed had previously served as treasurer for several years.

Later that year, in October 1938, Ed and Louise celebrated their 25th wedding anniversary at the Lake. As mentioned in the *Patchogue Advance*, among the relatives and friends were all four of Ed's siblings, as well as the couple's five children. "The couple were presented with a large silver-decorated wedding cake and the guests were entertained with games and several enjoyed the afternoon at the billiard table."

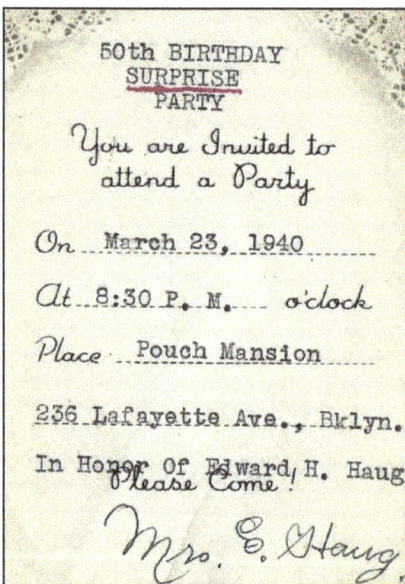

50th BIRTHDAY SURPRISE PARTY

You are Invited to attend a Party

On ___March 23, 1940___

At __8:30 P. M.___ o'clock

Place __Pouch Mansion__

__236 Lafayette Ave., Bklyn.__

In Honor Of Edward H. Haug

Please Come!

Mrs. E. Haug

Two years later in March 1940, Louise had a surprise party for Ed at the Pouch Mansion to celebrate his 50th birthday. As cited in the *Mid-Island Mail*, "Mr. Haug received a gold watch from the Square Club and his five children presented him with a power lawn mower as a birthday gift."

The year 1940 was also a federal census year. As recorded in that census, Ed and his brother Walter and their families were still living at 718 and 720 Herkimer St. and both were in the express business, transporting crates of shoes from the pier to various shoe stores around the city. Their homes were now valued at $3,000 each. Ed and Walter had worked 52 weeks and their salaries for the previous year were estimated to be $1,290 each (about $24,235 in 2021 dollars).

The 1930s had been a relatively peaceful decade for the country. That changed on December 7, 1941, when Japan bombed the U.S. fleet moored at Pearl Harbor, Hawaii. In a two hour surprise attack, Japanese warplanes sank or damaged 18 U.S. warships and destroyed 164 aircraft. Over 2,400 servicemen and civilians lost their lives that day. This was a seminal event that shifted the direction and resolve of the country. Every American who was alive at that time remembers that horrific attack.

Louise with her son Edward

January, 1942 - Gene and Edward Haug, Champaign, Illinois

By late 1942, all men ages 18-64 were required to register for the draft. Ed and Walter signed up on the same day, but realistically, only men under 38 years old were likely to be drafted. Two of the Haug boys, Edward and Gene, were drafted into the Army, as well as two future sons-in-laws, George Eckhardt and Elmer Ball, and Elmer served in the Pacific. It was a time of great stress and worry for every American – not knowing how long the war would last and if loved ones would return.

In April 1942, Edward Haug, Jr. was able to come home for a quick visit. His parents met him at LaGuardia Airport and he was reunited with family and friends out at the Lake. As mentioned in the *Patchogue Advance*, "Sergeant Haug flew home from Ft Knox, Kentucky, where he is an instructor in the armored tank school. His brother, Eugene, is an instructor at Chanute Field, Illinois and expects to fly home for a visit within the next two weeks."

The war brought immense changes to American life and required sacrifice and cooperation on the "Home Front." Rationing became part of everyday life and Americans learned to conserve all types of resources. Eating leftovers became a patriotic duty and civilians were urged to grow their own vegetables and fruit "victory gardens." To meet the military's need for metal, Americans held "scrap drives" around the nation and contributed old cars, bedframes, radiators, pots, pipes, etc. The U.S. military also faced a rubber shortage and needed millions of tires for jeeps, trucks and other vehicles. Therefore, the country imposed gas rationing and speed limits which forced people to reduce wear and tear and replacement of tires on their private automobiles.

Wedding photo - Marion and George Eckhardt, November 1, 1942

Ed could still get gas for Haug's Express (3 gallons per week) but he did not feel right about driving all the way out to Lake Ronkonkoma in light of the war restrictions. So he put up a sign at the refreshment stand saying it would be closed for the duration of the war. In 1944, Ed sold the stand, his deeded portion of the lake and the family's summer home to John Huth. The concession stand reopened from 1946-1964 and later became a small used book store.

It was still wartime when two of Ed and Louise's children got married, both in November 1942. Marion married her sweetheart, Corporal George Eckhardt, at St. John's Lutheran Church in Brooklyn and Gene married Dalice Schull in Biloxi, Mississippi. Before the end of the decade,

1955 - All 9 grandchildren: Back Row: Dalice Haug, Dorothy Haug, Grandpa holding Louise Eckhardt, Ruth Haug holding Joan Haug; Middle Row: Karen Haug, Edward Haug, George Eckhardt, Richard Ball; Front: Donald Haug on the tricycle.

daughter Ruth married Elmer Ball in 1946 and Edward Jr. married Ruth Newdoll in 1948. The oldest son, Henry, remained a confirmed bachelor until the age of 50 when he married a lovely German gal, Betty Jaax, in 1965.

Grandchildren soon followed and there would be nine in all. But sadly, Louise would not live long enough to meet the youngest ones. She had been diagnosed with Parkinson's disease and her health slowly declined. On April 13, 1953, she passed away at the age of 61. She and Ed had been married for almost 40 years.

Ed continued to work full-time at Haug's Express, but there were some major changes in the structure of the company.

When the business was first incorporated in March 1920, the brothers, Ed and Walter, each owned 49 shares and their wives owned one share each. In March 1949, Walter retired and sold his shares to Ed's son, Edward G. Haug — so father and son became the sole owners and jointly operated the business for several years.

At the same time, according to the company minutes, son Henry Haug resigned as Vice-President and Secretary. Edward G. Haug was elected his replacement. He would receive the weekly salary of $45.00. Edward H. Haug remained President and Treasurer of the company and received the same salary, $45.00 per week. The outstanding shares of stock were canceled and reissued with "right of survivorship" so that should either the President or Vice-President (Edward H. or Edward G. Haug) die, the stock would automatically revert to the survivor.

At the annual meeting in January 1955, Ed said he would retire as an officer of the corporation effective March 24, 1955 when he turned 65. A motion was passed that he would then be employed on a part-time basis to do clerical work at a salary of $50 per month. Mrs. Ruth Haug was voted in as Vice-President and Henry Haug as Secretary. In 1962, Mrs. Ruth Haug

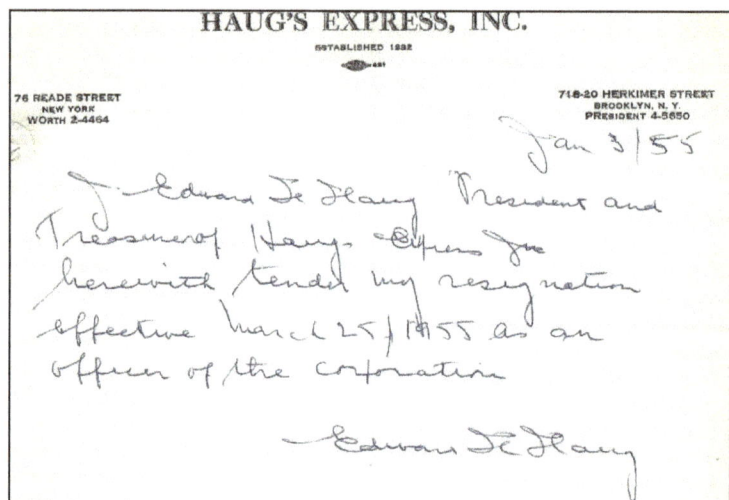

stepped down due to ill health and Eugene Haug took her place as Vice-President. In 1966, Eugene Haug resigned and Mrs. Virginia Haug took his place as Vice-President.

By the late 1960s, Haug's Express had five trucks. They bought a new one almost every year and just transferred the body (with the company lettering) onto the new chassis. Around 1970, Haug's Express merged with two other companies to become B.H.R. Hauling, Inc. (Bogen, Haug and Robbins). But even after the merger, Ed continued to be quite involved with the business. He would go over to the garage in Long Island City and help check-in drivers and make routes for the day. Haug's Express, which was started in 1882 by Ed's grandfather, had lasted as an independent business for almost 90 years.

In 1961, Ed was honored on his 71st birthday. A local paper described the event as "an unusual celebration and party . . . that was held in the old stable in the rear of his residence, 720 Herkimer St. The hayloft was beautifully decorated, a caterer provided a full course smorgasbord with a complete assortment of liquid refreshments. Music was provided for square and modern dancing. . . .A big surprise was the presence of the doctor who attended Mr. Haug at his birth 71 years ago. He is Dr. Longfellow, who traveled all the way from St. Petersburg, Florida for the occasion."

On his 75th birthday, Ed was honored again with a celebration at Durow's Restaurant. The *Ridgewood Times* said that "Mrs. Eckhardt introduced Benjamin Grindrod, lifelong friend of her father, who was master of ceremonies. Grindrod outlined the life of the honor guest during the past 60 years."

October 6, 1971 - Presentation of the 50th Year Masonic Award to Edward Haug with sons Edward (left) and Eugene (right)

Ed thoroughly enjoyed his retirement. Throughout the year there were always big family get-togethers for the major occasions – Father's Day, Thanksgiving, 4th of July, Birthday – rotated among his sons' and daughters' homes in Queens, Long Island and Staten Island. But best of all were those Christmas family get-togethers upstairs at 720 Herkimer St. and the exciting summer day at Steeplechase, Coney Island when Ed treated his entire family to a whole day of amusement rides and then dinner. Ed also made individual visits to his family – as well as trips to Florida (often with his sister, Eva) to spend time with his daughter, Ruth and her family, in Sarasota.

The famed Traymore Hotel in Atlantic City, NJ – demolished in 1972

In 1970, Ed was elected Monarch of the Long Island Grotto. He had always been very active in the Masons. As early as 1921, when he was 31 years old, he had attained the degree of Master Mason – the highest degree in Freemasonry. He was also a lifetime member of the Anglo-Saxon Lodge, No. 137, and Past President of the Ocean Hill Square Club.

As Monarch of the Long Island Grotto, Ed hosted a trip to Atlantic City. Many members of his family participated and we all stayed at the Traymore Hotel. My cousin Joan and   I had a wonderful time bike-riding on the boardwalk and horse-back riding on the beach. I remember that she and I could order anything on the menu for breakfast and our grandfather must have paid the tab later. We thought that was great – we felt like royalty!

Ed never remarried but he did have a girlfriend for many years, a widow named Mildred Keyes. She came to many of our family functions and was very kind and generous to all of Ed's grandchildren. And so was Ed. He always remembered all of our birthdays and Christmas with a card and savings bond – and each of his grandchildren received an uncirculated, mint $5.00 gold piece when we were confirmed.

When living in Bedford Stuyvesant started to became unsafe – Ed had been robbed a couple of times – he moved into an apartment in downtown Brooklyn in the same building as Mrs. Keyes. He had considered living on Staten Island but decided it was too country. He was much happier living in a high-rise apartment where he could happily look down at all the trucks and traffic in the streets below. He was a city person through and through!

Looking back, I realize that my grandfather was quite progressive. He was always a sharp dresser and when bell bottom pants, wide ties or long sideburns were in style – so was my grandfather. He always had the latest appliances too – a garbage disposal in the 1940s and one of the early color TVs in the 1960s. And long before it was common, he and his sister, Eva, went together for acupuncture treatments for their arthritis.

1971 - Edward Haug with his 5 children: Gene, Edward, Marion, Henry and Ruth

Whenever my grandfather visited my family on Staten Island, he used to bring me cigar bands which was great – for then I could order things from a catalogue like 45 RPM records. He did the same for my cousin Joan. And one time he brought me a pair of white go-go boots when they were in style and I was thrilled! I think I was about 10 years old at the time.

My cousin Ed said our grandfather taught him how to track stocks in the newspaper. He also taught him how to cook – because from living alone Grandpa had become quite a creative cook. At Haug's Express, Ed also said he learned to park vehicles – before he even learned to drive! Grandpa let him park the trucks in the garage and reposition them in the long driveway.

My brother, George, remembered how much Grandpa and Great-Aunt Eva loved to hear him play the accordion when he was a boy – especially old standard songs from days gone by. George played at family get-togethers and sometimes outside at Lake Ronkonkoma too. When George was older and part of a musical combo, Grandpa hired him to play at a few of his Masonic affairs as well.

On May 31, 1979, Grandpa Ed Haug passed away peacefully at the age of 89. My mother had been sitting with him in the hospital at the time writing a letter to me. He had fallen asleep and was snoring lightly. The room got quiet and when my mother looked up, she realized he had passed away.

My mother said he was not aware that he was in the hospital. He was looking forward to the upcoming get-together for Father's Day and what a nice time we would all have. My mother was so thankful that she had been there with him and that he had not died alone. And it gave her comfort to know that he had not been in pain and that he had died peacefully. As she wrote in her letter to me, "He died as he lived. He just took it in stride."

My mother said that Grandpa had a mirror that he intended to paint gold. He bought the paint and brush but never painted it – even though he had lived in his apartment for 11 years. So one time my mother asked him why he never painted the mirror and he said that was a project for when he got bored. After he died, my mother found the paint and brush so it was heartwarming for her to know that he must have never gotten bored.

In his will, Grandpa remembered his sister, Eva, with a $1,000 bond and Mrs. Keyes with a $500 bond. Each of his nine grandchildren received a $500 bond, as did his daughters-in-law and his sons-in-law. His five children received about $10,000 each after the estate was settled.

My Uncle Gene Haug was the executor of the estate. And In a letter to me when I was stationed overseas, he wrote that relatives and numerous friends had contributed $900 to the Masonic Home in my grandfather's name. "This is a remarkable tribute . . . and overwhelming evidence of the benevolent influence Grandpa had on those who knew him. We are left to strive to reach the goals of love, kindness and morality he has set for us through his life and actions."

My cousin, Dorothy, was unable to make the funeral, but in a letter to my mother, she said, "I'm sitting here thinking about Grandpa doing what everyone does when a loved one passes to a new life. . . . I can never recall any moments of meanness; just a warm caring man that was kept so busy trying to do for others and his family and his business. How many grandfathers took their grandkids to Steeplechase Park? How many grandfathers had a bag full of candy for the kids, parties at his house and ice cream till it came out of our ears! How many grandfathers showed up at all the important functions in the lives of his grandchildren and children? He did it all."

Grandpa Haug was a remarkable man who lived a very full and rich life. He had a positive impact on so many people through his kindness and generosity. He treated everyone fairly and truly lived by the tenets of Masonry: honesty, integrity and compassion for others. He was a prominent and well-respected businessman, but most important to him was Family. He was the focal point and the glue that held the family together and he was so proud and supportive of all of us.

My cousin, Edward Haug, probably summed it up best when he said, "Grandpa was the most amazing man I ever knew."

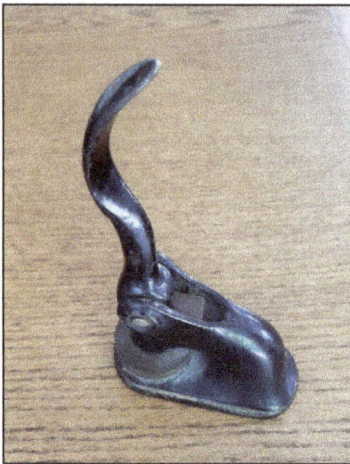

MOVING — STORAGE

Moving — Storage — Trucking

Haug's Express, Inc.

Serving You Since 1882

718-720 HERKIMER ST.

Brooklyn 33, N.Y.

Brooklyn Phone: Queens Phone:

PR. 4-5650   VI. 8-5802

Haug's Express corporate seal

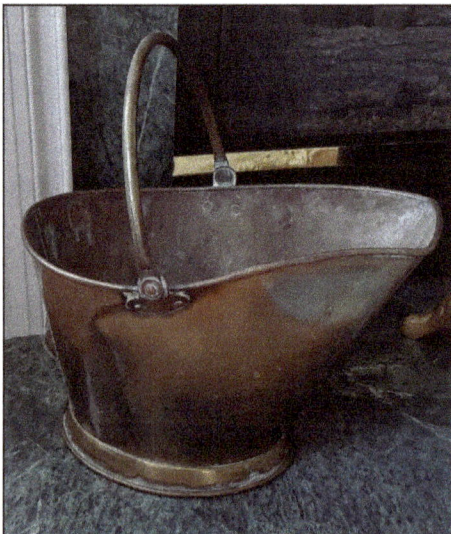

Coal skuttle from Haug's Express

Grandpa Haug's chest of drawers from when he was a boy

Louise Bachman

The Joseph & Katherine Bachman Family

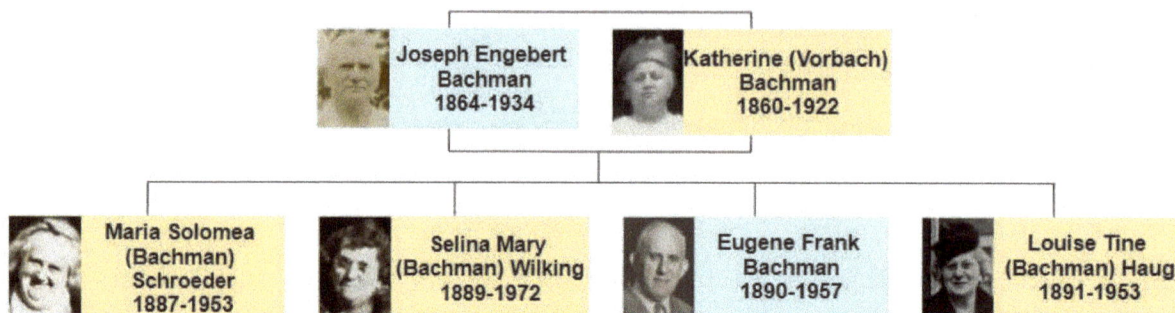

Joseph & Katherine Bachman

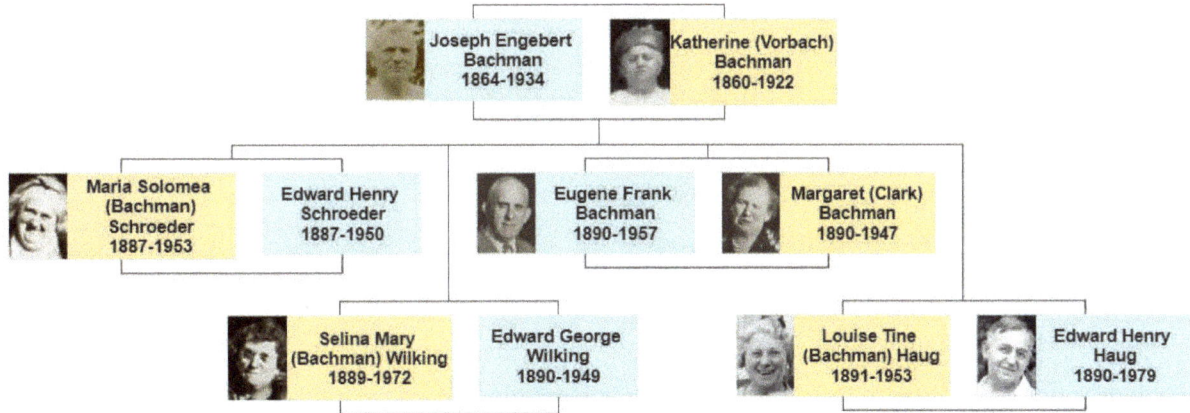

Joseph Engebert Bachman
1864-1934

Katherine (Vorbach) Bachman
1860-1922

Maria Solomea (Bachman) Schroeder
1887-1953

Edward Henry Schroeder
1887-1950

Eugene Frank Bachman
1890-1957

Margaret (Clark) Bachman
1890-1947

Selina Mary (Bachman) Wilking
1889-1972

Edward George Wilking
1890-1949

Louise Tine (Bachman) Haug
1891-1953

Edward Henry Haug
1890-1979

The Edward & Louise Haug Family

Henry & Edward Haug

Edward Henry
Haug
1890-1979

Louise Tine
(Bachman)
Haug
1891-1953

Henry Walter Haug
1915-1992

Barbara (Jaax)
Haug
1930-2007

Edward George
Haug
1917-2011

Ruth (Newdoll)
Haug
1916-1962

Virginia (Laube)
Reinhardt
Haug
1927-2017

Eugene Haug

Edward Henry Haug 1890-1979

Louise Tine (Bachman) Haug 1891-1953

Eugene Francis Haug 1918-1990

Dalice Ruby (Shull) Haug 1913-1943

Gladys (Hardman) Haug 1911-2012

Louise Christine Haug 1919-1920

Marion & Ruth Haug

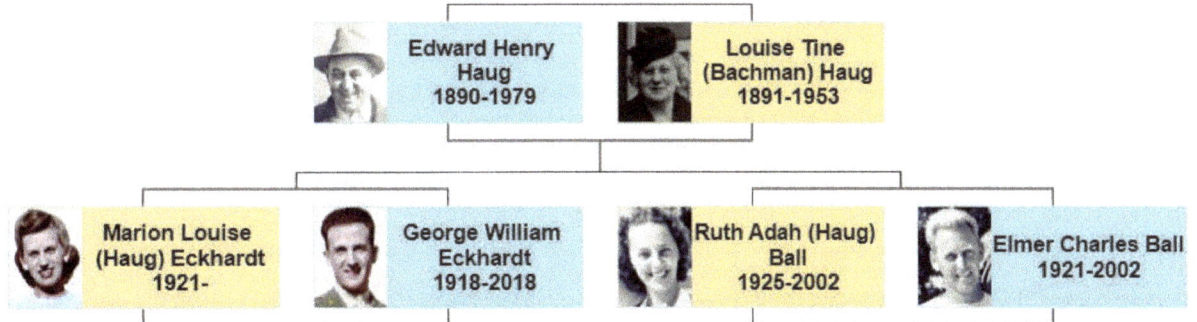

Edward Henry Haug 1890-1979

Louise Tine (Bachman) Haug 1891-1953

Marion Louise (Haug) Eckhardt 1921-

George William Eckhardt 1918-2018

Ruth Adah (Haug) Ball 1925-2002

Elmer Charles Ball 1921-2002

LOUISE TINE (BACHMAN) HAUG

"Whenever the place needed painting, we moved." That's what *my* mother said *her* mother said about her childhood – and it certainly seems to have been true. Little did the Bachmann family know what confusion this would create for a great-granddaughter who would be trying to pin down their history 120 years later!

I was named after my grandmother, Louise Bachman, but sadly, never had the opportunity to know her for she died two years before I was born. Louise appears to have been named after another Louise, but just who this woman was is still a mystery.

However, there are some things we do know for certain. Louise Tine Bachman was the fourth and youngest child of Joseph Engebert Bachman and Katherine Vorbach. Both parents had strong German backgrounds. Joseph emigrated from Bavaria, Germany, in 1872 with his mother when he was only 8 years old. Katherine's parents were also German immigrants. Therefore, it's not surprising that after Joseph and Katherine married in 1886, they continued to live in a German section of the Lower East Side of Manhattan in New York City. They then had four children in four years while living at three different addresses.

For many years prior to baby Louise's arrival, a number of relatives had lived in a tenement building at 217 East Fourth Street. When Louise was born on November 6, 1891, she was the fourth and last child of Katherine and Joseph. She had two older sisters: Maria (also known as Mamie) born in 1887 at 217 East Fourth Street and Salome (called Selina) born in 1889 at 526 Fifth Street. Louise also had an older brother, Eugene, born in 1890 at 191 Second Street in Manhattan.

Why did the Bachman family move so often? After so many years one can only speculate – but according to a long-standing custom that went back to colonial times, May 1st was the traditional moving day in New York City. A chronic housing shortage and high rents led tenants to move frequently in the hopes of improving their living conditions. On February 1st, landlords would notify their tenants as to what their new rent rate would be. On May 1st all leases expired in the city at exactly 9:00 AM. No trade was possible that day because of the traffic and gridlock in the streets – and pandemonium ensued as thousands of people scrambled to hire a cart or wagon to move all their worldly possessions to their new address. You can just imagine the noise, chaos and danger as thousands of horses, carriages and wagons hauled cargo up and down the streets in *any* direction – for it would be another decade before stop signs, traffic lights and traffic flow were implemented in the city.

May 1st – Moving Day in New York City

Wherever the Bachmans lived during the first several years of their marriage, they circled around the German section known as Kleindeutschland or "Little Germany." This was a very densely populated neighborhood – a 400-block area east of the Bowery, north of Division Street and south of 14th Street along the East River. Centered round Tompkins Square (known to the Germans as the Weisse Garten or "White Garden"), Kleindeutschland was a self-contained neighborhood.   Residents shopped in German-owned stores, attended German theaters, belonged to German clubs and frequented German beer halls. They probably shopped along Avenue B, known as the "German Broadway", the main commercial street. It was lined with small shops and basement factories where goods were piled everywhere on the canopied sidewalks. Close by was Avenue A, another busy street with many lager beer halls, oyster saloons and grocery stores.   People would also enjoy a stroll along the Bowery, the western border of Kleindeutschland and the center of culture and amusement with theaters, operas and beer "gartens."

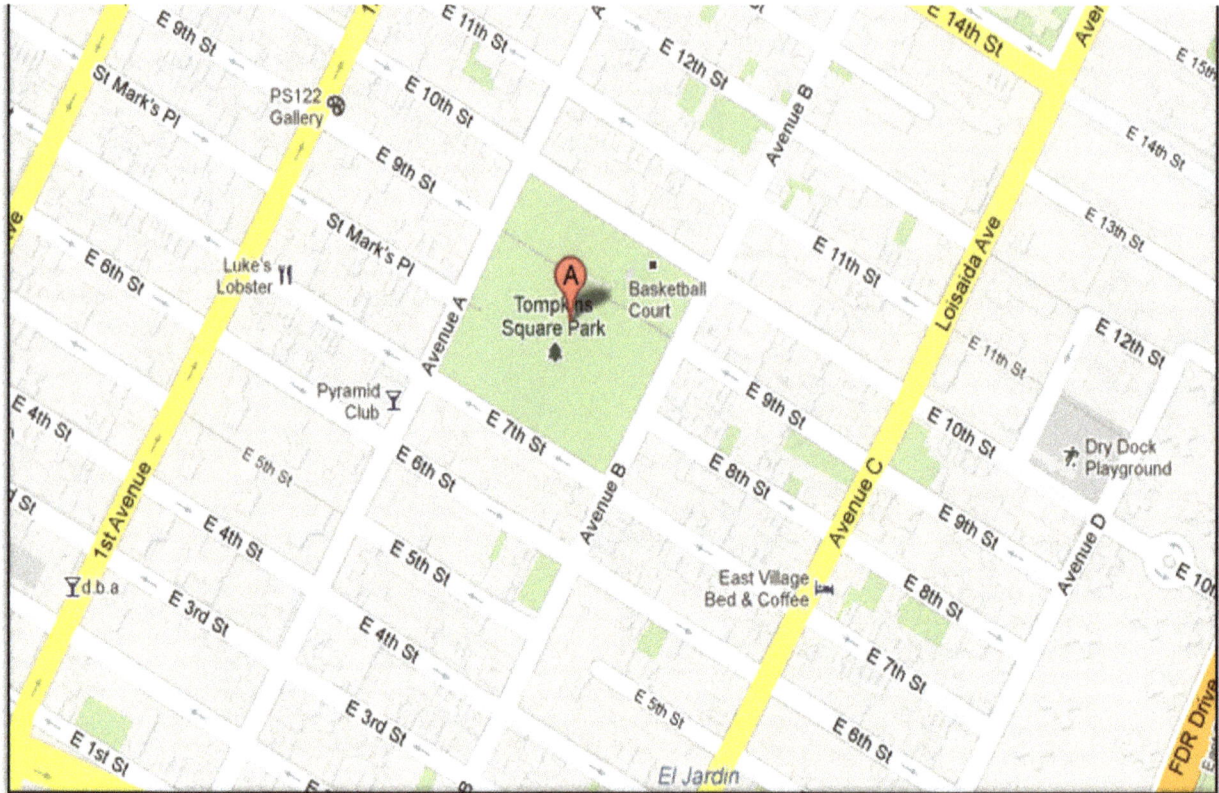

Kleindeutschland centered around Tompkins Square Park (from Google Maps)

German immigrants were known for their industriousness and were typically employed in manufacturing trades as skilled workers – tailors, carpenters, shoemakers, cabinet makers, bakers, cigar makers, butchers and makers of clocks and musical instruments. The community also had shopkeepers – grocers, peddlers, brewers, dry-goods dealers and saloon owners. Like many of his countrymen, Joseph Bachman worked in the needle trades – as an embroiderer, fringer, or a posamentier – a weaver of decorative trimming made of braid, lace or beads.

The church was central to the German way of life – and in the late 19th century there were four Catholic churches in Kleindeutschland. The Bachmann family attended the Church of Our Lady of Sorrows on Pitt and Stanton Streets. Established in 1867, this church still stands today - an ornate structure in the combined Victorian, Byzantine and Romanesque styles.

Church of Our Lady of Sorrows in Manhattan

Joseph Bachman and Katherine Vorbach were married August 22, 1886 in the Church of Our Lady of Sorrows. All four of their children were baptized there as well. According to baptism records, the three oldest children were named after a grandparent. And each child had two "sponsors" or godparents who were also grandparents. This was in keeping with a strong German tradition that considered godparents extremely important for providing food, shelter and education for the child if the parents were unable to. However, the youngest child was an exception. Baby Louise was baptized on November 15, 1891, and her sponsors were Henry Vorbach and Louise Vorbach. But just who these people were and how they were related is still a mystery.

Louise's mother, Katherine, had a brother named Henry so he could have been one of baby Louise's godparents. But who was Louise Vorbach? There was a young lady named Louise Vorbach, living in Manhattan at this time but her relationship to the Bachman family, if any, has not been established. Also, she was only 13 years old in 1891 so would Louise Bachman's parents have entrusted such a young person to be their baby's godparent? Whoever the Louise Vorbach on the baptism record was, she must have been a relative and an important person in the lives of Joseph and Katherine Bachman. In years to come the name "Louise" would be carried on to two of Louise Bachman's daughters: Louise and Marion Louise – as well as to two of her granddaughters: Dorothy Louise and to me. Hopefully, we will one day know the connection between Louise Bachmann and her godparent, Louise Vorbach.

Copied from the Church Baptism Register showing Louise's godparents, Henry and Louise Vorback

Today, virtually nothing is known about Louise's childhood except what can be imagined or surmised from the time and place in which she lived. And there are no extant photos of Louise as a young girl. As a toddler, her mother probably walked a few short blocks to let Louise frolic in the children's playground in Tomkins Square Park, just opened in 1894. She and her siblings must have had cousins and many friends to play with because the tenement buildings on the Lower East Side of Manhattan were crowded and teeming with people.

A typical tenement in Kleindeutschland was a large brick building, generally five or six stories tall. It was built on a lot fifty-feet wide and seventy-feet deep that held forty-eight apartments and at least that many families. Each floor had eight apartments, four facing the street and four facing the rear. Living conditions were cramped and crowded with very basic sanitation and poor ventilation – stifling hot in the summer and freezing cold in the winter. It wasn't unusual for people to seek relief from the oppressive heat by sleeping on fire escapes or the roofs of the buildings, but that involved another hazard – falling off.

A typical tenement in the Lower East Side of Manhattan

Perhaps it was these crowded conditions that prompted the Bachman family to pack up all their belongings and move again. By 1894 they had crossed the East River to live in Williamsburg – still an independent city and not yet part of a consolidated New York City. There they lived at 447 Grand Street in Williamsburg and a year later at 277 North 6th Street. Like Kleindeutschland in lower Manhattan, Williamsburg was a predominantly German area. But it was far from rural. Here the Bachmans were living about 10 blocks from the East River waterfront with its docks, shipyards, factories, distilleries, taverns, mills and foundries. This is also where some of the largest industrial firms in the nation had been built – like the Pfizer Pharmaceutical Company, Brooklyn Astral Oil (later Standard Oil) and Brooklyn Flint Glass (later Corning Glassware).In their new neighborhood, the Bachmans also had easy access to the Grand Street ferry that went back and forth across the river to the Lower East Side. So one can imagine the family did not feel completely removed from their relatives and all that had been familiar to them in Manhattan.

As the decade that became known as the "gay nineties" came to a close, the automobile or "horseless carriage" was just emerging. By the 1890s, electric streetcars had replaced horse drawn vehicles, running above or below ground to avoid the crowded streets. People were dancing the two-step to John Philip Sousa's marches and songs such as "The Sidewalks of New York" and "A Hot Time in the Old Town" were popular – as was a new form of syncopated piano playing known as ragtime. The Katzenjammer Kids with their German accents appeared in Sunday comic pages. But the newspapers in 1900 made no mention yet of words such as "radio" or "movie" for they were unheard of at this time and still several years in the future.

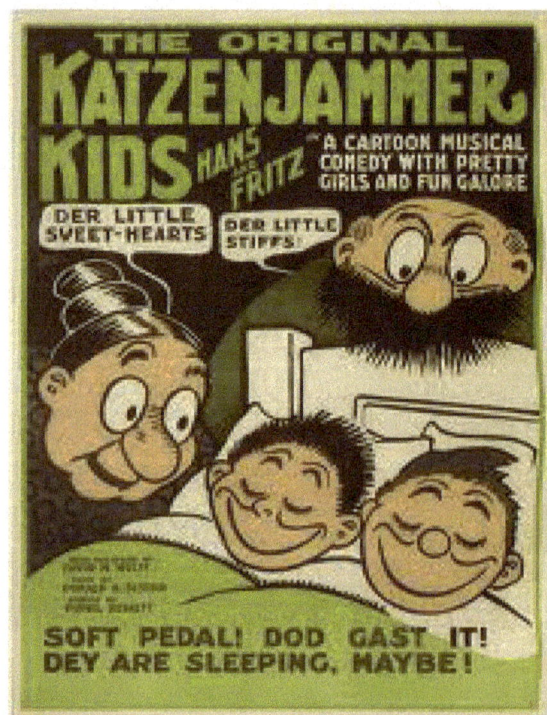

By 1900 the family had moved once again – further north to 259 Evergreen Ave. and to another German area in the adjoining section of Bushwick, Brooklyn. Louise was now 9 years old and attending school, along with her brother and sisters. Like typical schoolgirls her age she probably wore a shirtwaist and skirt or dresses that had a low waist line and covered her knees. Children at this time seldom had schooling past the 12th grade.

In the early years of this new century, one can easily imagine the Bachman family swept up in the excitement of a momentous event – the opening of the Williamsburg Bridge in December 1903. This engineering marvel was the second bridge to span the East River between Brooklyn and Manhattan and the longest suspension bridge built at that time. Having just turned 12 years old, Louise must have been keenly aware of this exciting event. As *The New York Times* described the scene, enormous and enthusiastic crowds on both sides of the river flocked to see the illumination of the giant span at night, the fireworks display and the brilliant marine pageant. The following day there were parades and marching bands and "the crowds cheered uproariously amid the thunder of cannon." A huge American flag was unfurled on each of the towers and Mayor Low pronounced the new Williamsburg Bridge open to public use. What an exciting time and memorable event this must have been for Louise and her family!

Postcard of Williamsburg Bridge, opened December 19, 1903, crossing the East River from Delancey Street, Manhattan to Broadway, Brooklyn

By 1905, the Bachmans were still living in Bushwick, Brooklyn, but they had moved again – this time to 400 Bleecker Street. Louise and her brother, now 13 and 14 respectively, were still in school but their older sisters were not. Mamie, age 17, was engaged in the same posamentary needlework as her father and Selina, age 16, was doing housework according to the 1905 city census.

Five years later, both Louise and her brother had also joined the work force. Louise (or "Tina L" as recorded in the 1910 census) was a "joiner" working with druggist supplies and Eugene was an apprentice in a machine shop. Their sister Selina was a seamstress making shirtwaists. The family had not moved far but they were now living in the Ridgewood section of Queens. This area was traditionally home to a large community of German immigrants who worked in the breweries and knitting factories that straddled the Queens-Brooklyn border.

Right across the street from their home at 74 Foxall Street, the Bachmans probably attended the St. Matthias Roman Catholic Church at 73 Foxall Street. In April, 1911, Selina was the first of the four Bachmann children to marry. Selina tied the knot with Edward George Wilking at that same church and her siblings, Mamie and Eugene, were the witnesses to the happy event.

Edward Haug, the expressman

Within the next year Louise also had a beau, a young man she had met at work. Edward Henry Haug was an expressman who transported freight around the city by horse and wagon. He used to stop by Louise's place of work every day to pick up shipments (of shoes primarily) where she worked as a forelady in a factory. In the only surviving letter from their courtship days, "Eddie" expressed his concern that Louise was sick and he had brought her a bottle of oil of camphor, his recommended remedy for a sore throat, along with cough drops and cold water. But he had missed seeing her. That's when he was sure she must be home sick – plus he had heard from his brother that she would not be able to attend an upcoming tea party. He signed the letter, "Yours Forever, Eddie" with three kisses, "XXX. "Clearly, he was smitten.

Eddie's charms must have worked on "Weezie" as he affectionately called her – for a year and a half later, on September 29, 1913, the couple applied for a marriage license. Louise was 21 years old, living at 1815 Gates Avenue in Ridgewood, Queens. Eddie was 23, living at 119 Marion Street in Brooklyn. They married three weeks later on October 19, at St. Brigids Rectory in Brooklyn in a Catholic ceremony. One has to wonder if the difference in their religions caused disapproval in their families – for this was a much bigger issue 100 years ago than it is today. Nevertheless, the couple had a church wedding and Louise's sister, Mamie, and Eddie's brother, Walter, were the witnesses. The couple then spent their honeymoon in Baltimore and stayed with Eddie's father's relatives.

Louise and Eddie's wedding photo, October, 1913

Louise and Eddie settled down in the Bedford Stuyvesant section of Brooklyn. They lived right next door to Eddie's mother, brother, and two sisters on Marion Street. Around the corner was Haug's Express, the family business with its stable entrance on Patchen Ave. This delivery business had been started by Eddie's father in 1882 and taken over by Eddie and his brother, Walter, after the death of their father in 1910.

Although Louise and Eddie were different religions, they decided to raise their family as Protestant. Or perhaps this was just the logical path because Eddie and his family had been residents and businessmen in that neighborhood for decades, as well as members of the local church.

In any event, when their first child was born in January, 1915, baby Henry was baptized in the Protestant Herkimer Street German Reformed Church. Eddie had also been baptized and confirmed in this church and his family had been members for over 35 years. But Louise's sister, Mamie, did not approve. As the family story goes, she scooped up little Henry and dashed him off to a Catholic church to be baptized properly! A few years later, Louise gave birth to two more sons – Edward in 1917 and Eugene in 1918.

Louise with a happy baby Henry

The addition of two more sons to the family, Edward and Eugene

But despite the joys of raising a family, the ongoing war in Europe and the looming threat of American involvement must have caused tremendous concern. President Wilson had attempted to keep the U.S. neutral but with the sinking of the Lusitania and all-out submarine warfare against American ships, the U.S. entered World War I in April, 1917. Eddie was eventually exempt from military service. But Louise must have been terribly worried about her brother Eugene. For over a year he was stationed overseas in Europe serving in the Army infantry.

In 1917, there was another noteworthy event for the Haug family – the purchase of the first automobile! At a time when autos were just beginning to replace the horse and buggy, Eddie's sister, Eva, bought a Ford Model-T touring car for $381.00 – which included $8.00 for the horn and $20.00 for the "demountable rims." Also known as the "Tin Lizzie," this car must have been black because as Henry Ford reportedly said, "You can have any color you want, as long as it's black." How exciting this must have been for the entire family because Eva let her brothers borrow the car for family excursions and outings to the beach. You can just picture Eddie cranking up the car with Louise and the little boys inside waiting impatiently for this great adventure to begin. And driving an automobile anywhere in 1917 was certainly an adventure – over dirt and muddy roads at a top speed of 45 mph.

Visiting Eddie's sister, Henrietta Wecht, in Port Jervis, NY – Louise (sitting), Edward Jr. (standing on the running board), Henry (sitting over the tire), Eugene (sitting on the door), Henrietta Bermel (Eddie's mother is standing) and Eddie and Frank Wecht

In 1918, on the 11th hour of the 11th day of the 11th month, Germany and the Allies signed the armistice that ended World War I. Louise must have been so relieved when her brother returned from the battlefields of Western Europe. Eugene was honorably discharged in April, 1919.

More good news followed just a few months later when Louise found out she would be having another child. The couple's first daughter, Louise, was born shortly before Christmas, 1919. But sadly, the child would live only 6 months. Her distraught parents had been advised to take their ailing daughter to the seashore to convalesce but she died in the train on the way home. Baby Louise died of pneumonia on June 24, 1920, and her parents were devastated. Many years later,

Louise's son, Edward, still remembered his mother crying all the time even though he had been just a young child when his baby sister died.

Death certificate of baby Louise who died at the age of 6 months

By 1920, according to the federal census, Edward and Louise, just 29 and 28 years old, owned their home at 119 Marion St. Upstairs they rented two apartments: Edward's mother lived on the top floor and his sister, Marguerite Ewing, and her husband, George, lived on the second floor.

In the 1920s, the birth of two more daughters completed the family so now there were five children in all. Marion Louise was born in 1921 and oddly enough, was named after the street where they lived.

Marion and Gene (front row), Edward (left) and Henry (back row)

Louise and Henry (back row), Edward, (left) Marion (center) and Gene

Ruth – the youngest child, beside Marion, Gene, Edward and Henry, (1926)

The youngest child, Ruth Adah, was born in 1925. Although 3 ½ years apart, the two girls were always close and many family photos show them posing together. As long as they lived, the two sisters talked on the phone every Saturday like clockwork and remained close even though they lived 1,200 miles apart.

So it was a busy and happy household with five active children and various cousins, aunts and uncles frequently dropping by. Louise certainly had her hands full running the household and helping with Haug's Express at the same time.

Louise was an excellent business woman in her own right, according to her daughters. And she was a tremendous asset to Haug's Express. She took typing lessons (at 50 cents per lesson) to handle the correspondence. She also paid the bills and answered the telephone – and with her feisty personality, it's not hard to imagine her interacting and kibitzing with the customers and truck drivers. However, the drivers were also very respectful toward her. In between, she kept a watchful eye over five children.

At home, Louise ran a tight ship and was the disciplinarian of the household. The house was spotless and her daughter Ruth said you couldn't leave anything lying around or it would get thrown out. Besides making six beds every day, Louise scrubbed the floors on her hands and knees. She also cooked big meals with great big pots, never knowing how many people would show up for lunch or dinner. On Sunday, Louise would usually cook a large roast with fried potatoes and there was always plenty of food for any friends or relatives that might unexpectedly drop by. She was an excellent cook and some of her popular dishes were sauerbraten and potato balls, homemade noodles and bread pudding. All the children knew they had to be home by 6:00 sharp for dinner – and their father ate later whenever he returned from work.

Louise and the girls, Marion (left) and Ruth

For relaxation, Louise loved to sew or crochet while listening to her favorite programs on the radio. She had learned to crochet from her mother-in-law and eventually crocheted bedspreads for every bed in the house.

Around 1922, the Haug family packed up and moved a few blocks away to live next door to Edward's brother, Walter. Edward and Walter jointly purchased two attached brick buildings, 25'x100' and the two Haug families lived side-by-side at 718 and 720 Herkimer St. in Brooklyn.

The previous owner, Al Culliford, had had a livery business there and the basement was equipped to hold 40 horses. In back was a large two-story garage to store the wagons so this was an ideal location for the expanding express business.

But 1922 was also a sad year. Louise's mother, Katherine, died of liver cancer at the age of 62 after lapsing into a coma. It appears Louise took care of her during her final days because she died at 718 Herkimer St. although this was not her home address.

The Casino

In 1924, Eddie and Louise, with the five little Haugs in tow, visited Lake Ronkonkoma, a popular Long Island summer resort. Leaving the stifling hot asphalt of the city to swim in the cool waters of the lake must have been delightful. So the Haugs decided to spend the summer and stayed at the Lake Front Hotel. The next summer they rented a large house with six bedrooms facing the Lake called "The Casino." With an option to buy, Eddie purchased the house for $9,000 the following year. Thereafter, the Haug family spent many wonderful summers at Lake Ronkonkoma while Eddie traveled back and forth on weekends so he could continue to run the express business in Brooklyn.

Lake Ronkonkoma had become a popular resort for the wealthy and famous from New York City, especially after the Vanderbilt Parkway was built (also known as the Long Island Motor Parkway). Privately funded by William K. Vanderbilt II, an auto racing enthusiast, and other financiers, the Vanderbilt Parkway was the first roadway designed for automobile use only – so it would be free of dust churned up by horses. Originally intended for racing, this highway had banked turns, guard rails, reinforced concrete, and bridges and overpasses to eliminate intersections. By 1911 when the road was extended to Lake Ronkonkoma, New York City, residents could motor 48 miles along this toll road from Queens to their summer estates on Long Island. During Prohibition, the Vanderbilt Parkway was also known as "Rumrunners Road" because bootleggers often used it to outrun the police.

In the 1920s and 1930s, Lake Ronkonkoma was really hopping – especially during Prohibition. A colorful local figure was a man named Jack Brown who ran a tavern – a lively place with a swinging band that could be heard by the Haugs who lived right next door. Jack Brown was quite a character and his tavern was frequented by popular celebrities of the day like Betty Boop, George Burns and Roy Rogers *with* his white horse, according to son Henry Haug. Jack called Henry, "Kid," and would sometimes let him ride around in his Pierce Arrow automobile when Henry was about 12. According to Henry, Jack Brown was a very nice man who loved to play the trombone in his own band and when he'd been drinking, he usually played his favorite song, "Roses of Picardy." Henry said Jack was a kingpin of the bootleg era. He got booze from Canada and stored it in bathhouses before selling it to locals or serving it in his tavern – and there was plenty of alcohol, despite Prohibition.

Jack Brown's Tavern in the mid-1930s (Photo from Lake Ronkonkoma by Keith Oswald and Dale Spencer). You can see "The Casino" on the right.

During the day, visitors to the lake could enjoy bathing in the cool, sparkling water, fishing, canoeing or row boating. There were also motorboat races and excursion boats that circled the two-mile lake. At night, guests could dance, listen to jazz bands or gamble in the casinos in several pavilions that lined the lakefront. On the 4th of July, huge crowds flocked to the area to see fireworks on a barge in the middle of the lake. Another popular attraction was a local guy named Jimmy Horning who would parachute into the lake on Saturdays, Sundays and holidays and then pass the hat for donations. It was unusual and considered quite a feat – particularly one time when he missed the lake, landed in a tree and had to be rescued.

The family refreshment stand, "Haug's Casino"

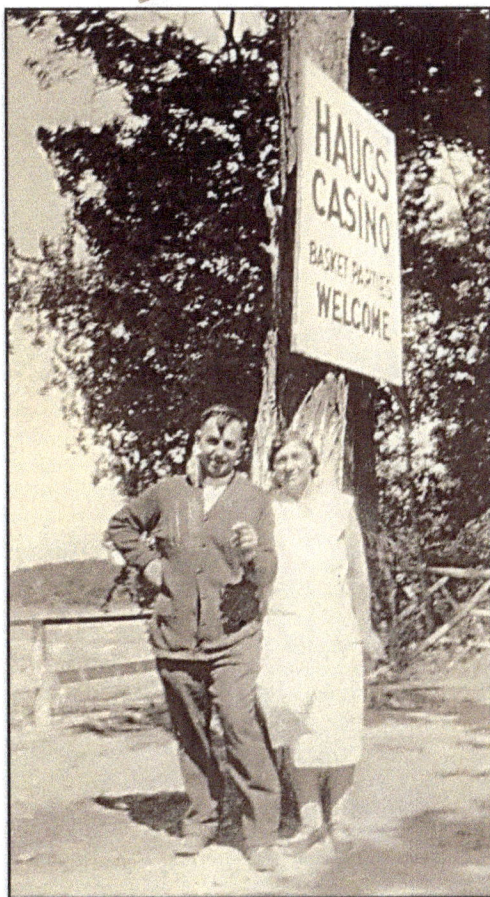

Louise and Eddie

People who intended to spend the day swimming in Lake Ronkonkoma faced an obstacle though. Bathers were only allowed access to the beach and lake if they owned the land beneath the lake. A man in a rowboat even circled the lake to chase trespassers away. So Eddie purchased a parcel of land for $1800 that extended 250' underneath the lake for $20 per foot.

He had a refreshment stand built across the road from their house. Then he bought the bathhouses from Olympia Pavilion and had them floated over to the beach area near the stand. The Haugs called their business "Haug's Casino." It was a family affair – a clever move designed to keep all five children occupied for the summer and out of mischief. Sons Eddie Jr. and Gene ran the refreshment stand that sold candy and soda and eventually hamburgers, hot dogs, clam chowder and cold beer. Marion and Ruth were locker girls in charge of the bathhouses that you could rent for $5.00 per locker for the season – while Henry parked cars for 50 cents each. And behind the scenes Louise kept the roadside stand supplied with burgers and chowder.

Louise and Eddie enjoying the beach, (1927)

Ruth and Marion with watchful parents in the background, (1928)

The summers spent at Lake Ronkonkoma were a magical time for the whole Haug family and collectively, they have many fond memories. All the children developed life-long friendships and both daughters met their future husbands there as well.

1928 - At the Lake, Ruth, Marion, Gene, Edward, Henry

But summers inevitably come to an end so life resumed in Brooklyn. By 1930, Louise and Eddie owned their own home at 718 Herkimer St. and it was worth $25,000. They also owned a radio, as mentioned in the 1930 census. Louise loved listening to her radio and had it playing all day. Upstairs, lived Louise's sister, Mamie, who enjoyed gazing out the window and watching all the activity below. She was a large woman and when she died several years later, she had to be hoisted out of the house by piano movers.

Louise's other sister, Selina, had moved to Philadelphia so the Haug family would pile in the car and drive there for Thanksgiving. This was a big trip – about 100 miles – especially for Ruth who usually got carsick. Marion and Ruth sat in the jump seats behind their mother and father so they were facing the three boys. Of course there was always fighting and bickering and their mom would turn around and swat the kids when they misbehaved.

Car trips took much longer then and inevitably one of the kids would have to go to the bathroom en route. So Eddie had a hole drilled in the floor of the car with a funnel and a seat on top which served as a make-shift rolling bathroom. According to son Edward, one time a car passed and told them that water was leaking from the car. Eddie thanked the man and they drove merrily on their way.

After such a big trip, the family would stay overnight – and Marion remembers that all five kids would sleep in one bed crossways. Aunt Selina's house was unusual in that it offered little privacy. There was a bathroom in the kitchen but no door, just a curtain. And upstairs the tub was in a hallway by itself and you had to pass through a room to get to it.

Louise (left) with her two sisters, Mamie (center) and Selina

Louise and Eddie had a busy social life. Louise belonged to the Order of the Eastern Star and Eddie was a Master Mason and President of the Ocean Hill Square Club so they often went out with friends and relatives. But Louise drew the line on some social functions. One time Eddie took Louise to a vaudeville show that had nude or scantily clad women. Louise walked out.

Another time they went to the opera and their daughter Marion, who was about 12 years old at the time, got a fit of giggling with her friend every time the fat opera singer opened her mouth and sang, "Ha, Ha, Ha." Her mother, who was sitting behind her, kept hitting Marion in the head but to no avail – she couldn't stop giggling. By the time they got home, Marion had developed a sharp pain in her abdomen. She had burst appendix, a very serious medical emergency, especially in the 1930s. Her parents called for an ambulance and in the rush to get Marion to the hospital, Louise tossed her rings on the dresser. They were stolen that night when someone broke into the house. The thief was never found – but fortunately, Marion made a full recovery after the removal of her appendix.

In 1935, Eddie decided to try his hand at local politics. Louise was not crazy about the idea. Nevertheless, he ran for alderman, a position similar to a councilman and elected by the people of a particular district. Ultimately, Eddie lost against his Democratic opponent, John Cashmore, who went on to become the borough president of Brooklyn. Later, when there was a kidnapping attempt on Cashmore's son, Louise was even more relieved that Eddie had lost the election and never entered politics.

October 19, 1938 marked Louise and Eddie's 25th wedding anniversary. They celebrated at the Lake with many friends and relatives including all five children and Eddie's brother and sisters. The couple was presented with a large silver-decorated wedding cake and the guests were entertained with games and an afternoon at the billiard table. The couple also received a beautiful silver, three-tier serving tray that is unique because it folds and takes up very little space.

Louise's Eastern Star pin that she wore often.

ELECT
For Alderman
48th Aldermanic Dist.   5th Assembly Dist.

23

EDWARD
HAUG ⬮ 177
Regular Republican Candidate

Eddie gave Louise a stunning diamond and pearl ring for their anniversary. He had had the diamond removed from an antique stick pin and then paid $10 each for eight pearls that surround the diamond. This ring was passed down to Louise's daughter, Marion, who enjoyed wearing it for many years – until she gave it to me because I had always admired it. Now I've worn the ring for many years and treasure it for its unique design and family history.

Eddie gave Louise this pearl and diamond ring on their 25th anniversary

Another anniversary gift – a folding silver tray

Sadly, about this time Louise started showing symptoms of what was eventually diagnosed as Parkinson's – a disease not well understood in the late 1930s. Treatment was primitive and ineffective. The doctors encouraged her to smoke menthol cigarettes so she and her daughter, Marion, would puff away. It was also recommended that she drink champagne. The doctors thought Louise's gold-capped teeth might have something to do with the disease too so she had all her teeth removed and replaced with false teeth. Of course this was painful and pointless. She also had to take medicine that made her awfully sick – much of it was experimental and probably did more harm than good. None of these "remedies" were helpful. For the rest of her life, Louise suffered from Parkinson's and her health declined as the disease gradually took its toll on her strength and energy.

Marion and George Eckhardt at his parent's home in South Ozone Park, Queens

But perhaps Louise's spirits were lifted when two of her children got married in November 1942. Marion married her childhood sweetheart from Lake Ronkonkoma, George Eckhardt, on the 1st of November. It was wartime and George was home on leave so they did not have a fancy wedding. Marion's sister, Ruth, was maid-of-honor and hobbled down the aisle on crutches. She had broken her leg in a horse-back riding accident. Eugene was married at the end of November – to Dalice Shull, a girl he met while stationed in Biloxi, Mississippi.

This was during World War II when thousands of men were drafted for military service to try and stop Hitler's march across Europe. Edward Jr. was the first of Louise's sons to go into the Army. Understandably, she was very upset. No one knew what to expect or how long the war would drag on. The day Edward left everyone was sleeping so he walked out of the house quickly without saying good-bye.

After about 10 months of service, Edward was able to fly home on leave from Ft. Knox, Kentucky where he was an instructor in the armored tank school. His parents met him at LaGuardia Airport and they drove out to Lake Ronkonkoma where a party of excited friends and relatives were there to greet him. However, his brother Eugene could not attend because by then he too was in the Army and an instructor at Chanute Field, Illinois. And son-in-law George Eckhardt was also away serving in the Army Air Corps as a physical therapist at Langley Field, Virginia.

April 1942 – Eddie Jr. home on leave from WWII. Photo taken at Herkimer St. Brooklyn

Jan 15, 1942 – Gene and Eddie at Chanute Field, Champaign, Illinois

In the summer of 1943, Louise and her daughter, Ruth, boarded a train to visit Marion and George in Buckroe Beach, Virginia. They had a grand time – even though Marion and George were living in nothing more than a cold-water shack that had been a bathhouse converted to a bungalow. A few mice inhabited the place too – but nevertheless, Louise and Ruth had a wonderful time.

In December 1943, Louise and Eddie received joyous news. They were grandparents for the first time. Gene's wife, Dalice, had given birth to twin girls in Elmira, New York. Although Gene was still in the Army and unable to be with his wife, they did speak on the phone, shared the wonderful news, and named the babies Dorothy and Dalice. Tragically, this was the last conversation they ever had. Dalice died of blood clots in her lungs a few days later – and the family was in shock.

July 1943 – Louise at Buckroe Beach, Virginia

At first, a woman named Mrs. Betty Lane, (in Elmira, New York), took care of the twins – while their father tried, unsuccessfully, to get discharged from the Army. Eventually, Gene and the twins were reunited and they moved in with Louise and Eddie on Herkimer St. So Gene was a single Dad, and his mother took care of the twins all day while he went to work. But it was a difficult situation and Louise was not well. Sometimes she would get a little break when Henry drove her and the twins over to Marion and George's house on Ralph Ave. which was about three blocks away. But more often, Gene would just drop the twins off with Marion for the day, (along with the dog), which allowed Louise to get some rest.

In February, 1947, Ruth married her long-time beau from Lake Ronkonkoma, Elmer Ball. And a year later, Edward Jr. married another Brooklyn gal, Ruth Newdoll. The oldest son, Henry, would remain a confirmed bachelor for 50 years until he married a German girl, Barbara Jaax – but this was long after Louise had passed away.

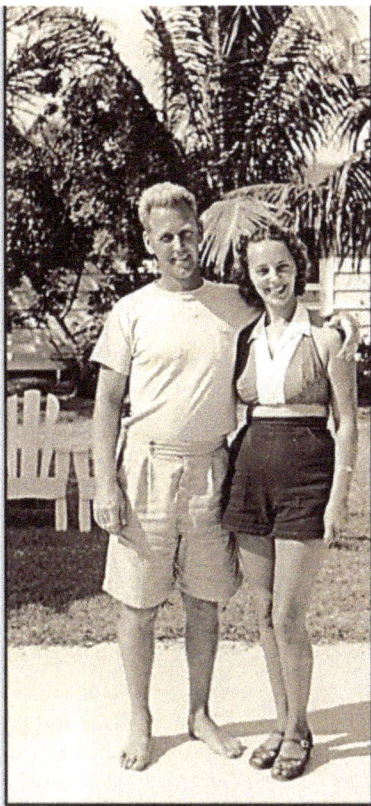

Ruth and Elmer Ball – photo taken in Sarasota, Florida where they lived for many years

Fortunately, Louise did live long enough to welcome several more grandchildren into the world: George Eckhardt (September 1947), Richard Ball (February 1949), and two of Edward's children; Karen (December 1949) and Edward III (April 1952). Eugene eventually remarried in 1950 and he and Gladys Hardman also had a son, Donald, born May 1952.

A very small religious medal that Louise treasured

The close ties of her expanding family must have offered some solace to Louise as her health continued to decline. She passed away on April 13, 1953, at her home in Brooklyn at the age of 61.Toward the end when she was very ill, Louise questioned whether she was being punished for abandoning her faith. And although Marion offered to call a priest for her, she declined. Louise never spoke about her religion but she did keep one very small Catholic medal – and one has to wonder whether she always felt guilty for marrying outside her faith.

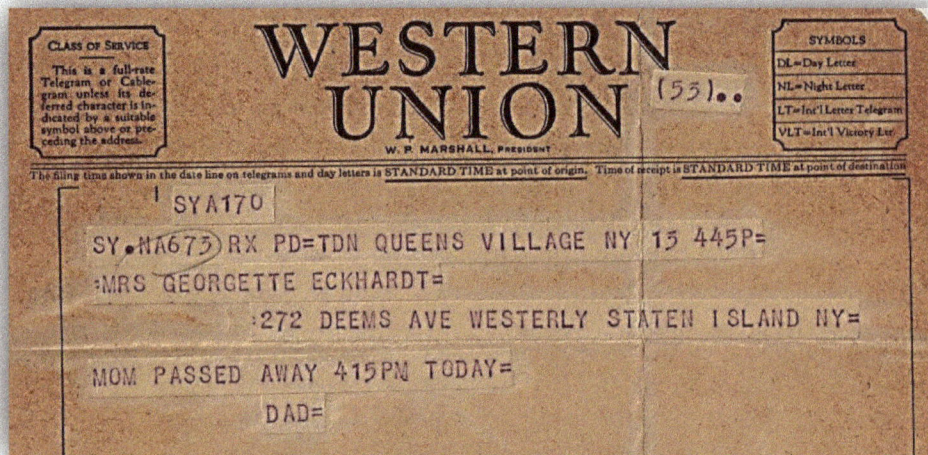

Louise Tine Haug is buried beside her husband, Edward Haug, in Evergreen Cemetery in Brooklyn, New York.

My favorite photo – Happy times at Atlantic City, New Jersey with Marion and Ruth

"

A carved wooden box that belonged to Louise

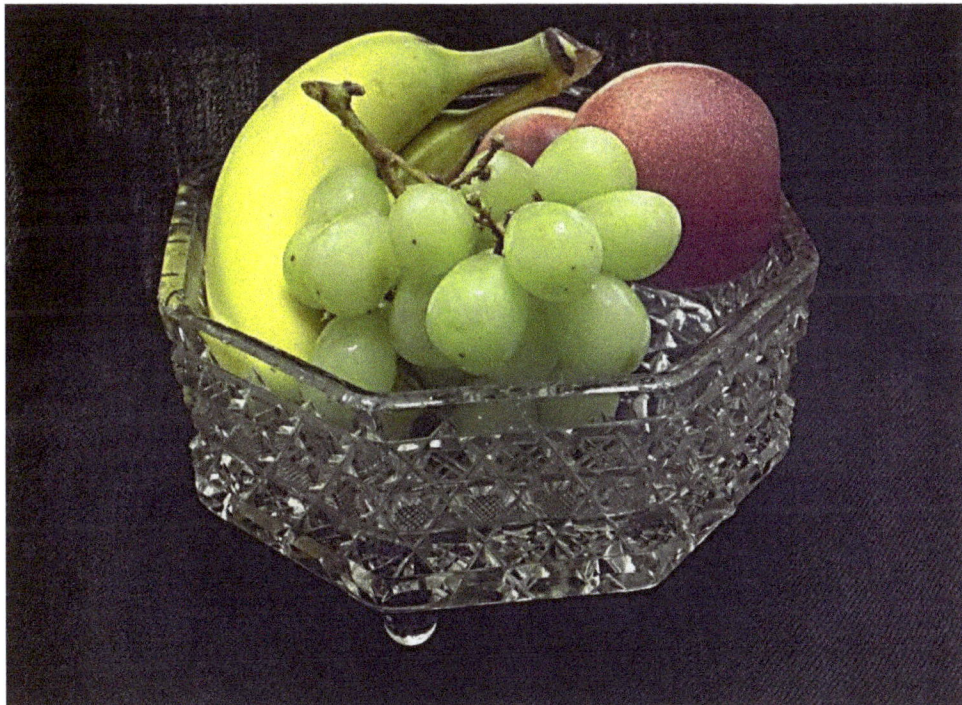

A cut-glass bowl that Louise normally kept in the kitchen filled with fruit

Louise's porcelain vase marked "Made in Austira, Royal Wettina"

Eva (Haug) Lenning

The Henry & Eva Haug Family

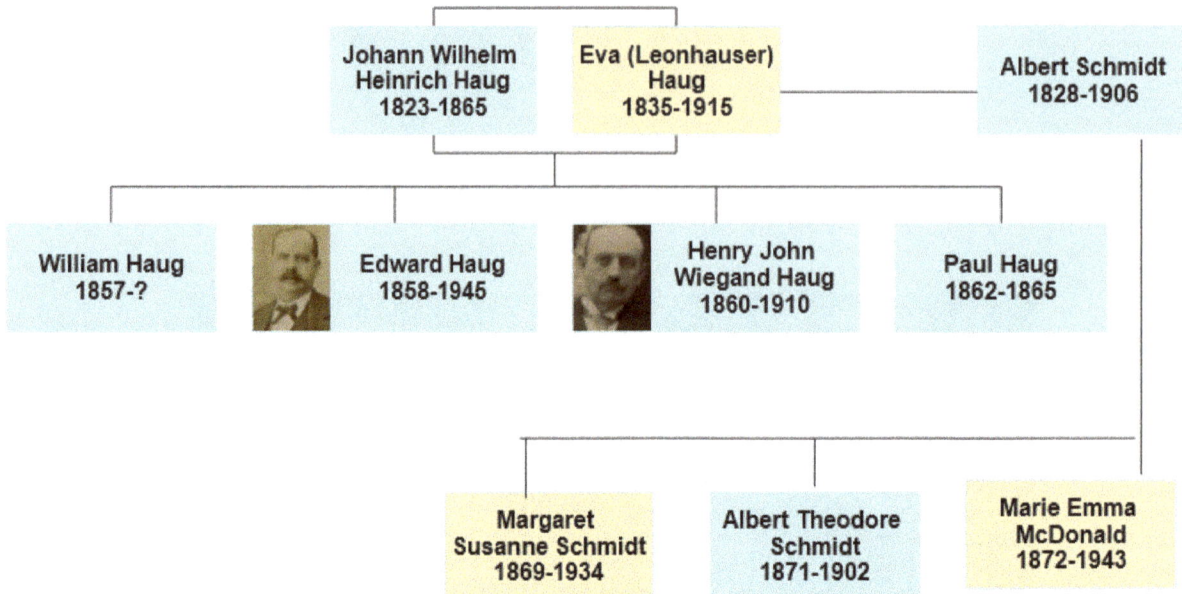

The Henry & Henrietta Haug Family

Henry John
Wiegand Haug
1860-1910

Henrietta Bermel
1862-1934

Eva (Haug)
Lenning
1885-1984

Henrietta (Haug)
Wecht
1888-1971

Edward Henry
Haug
1890-1979

Walter John Haug
1892-1955

Marguerite Anna
(Haug) Ewing
1896-1981

Eva & Henrietta Haug

Edward, Walter & Marguerite Haug

Eva (Haug) Lenning

My great-aunt Eva was an amazing person and she lived a long and remarkable life. She was extremely family-oriented and keenly interested in learning about her ancestors. Fortunately for her descendants, she wrote "The Henry Haug Story," when she was in her mid-nineties. It's a wonderful and descriptive account of the Haug family and Eva's fond memories of growing up in Brooklyn. What she wrote is invaluable and had it not been for her, much of this family information would probably have been lost to history. To pay homage to her, here is a slightly edited version of what she wrote with additional comments and photos that hopefully enhance her story and help portray her remarkable life. (Louise Eckhardt)

THE HENRY HAUG STORY

By Eva Haug Lenning

Over a hundred years ago, our Grandpa Henry Haug and his wife lived in a little town called Catonsville outside of Baltimore. Grandma's name was Eva. Grandpa taught school in the little schoolhouse and took charge of the choir in the church. He also gave voice lessons, sang solos himself and often had to conduct in church when the minister was absent.

LE: Johann Wilhelm Heinrich Haug was his name. He was born April 24, 1823, in the Kingdom of Wurttemberg in what is now Neuweiler, Calw, Germany. He immigrated to the United States around 1852 and became a member of The Old Salem Lutheran Church in Catonsville, Maryland, a church that was built by German Lutheran immigrants. According to the church minutes: "Mr. Haug was the new teacher and on July 27, 1863, school began again. The new teacher was given the keys of the parish and to the organ. He was to ring the bell and play the organ, besides teach."

Henry Haug had two sons, Edward and Henry. He died at a very young age and is buried in the churchyard cemetery, which is still there. The old brick church is also still standing and is used for functions for they now have a large church.

LE: William (also known as Henry) died in 1865 and is buried in the cemetery adjacent to the Old Salem Lutheran Church. He was 42 years old.

Prior to his death, the "Houck" family appeared in the 1860 federal census living in the First Ward of Baltimore City. "William" was 36 years old and a school teacher, Eva was 24 and their three sons were ages 3, 2 and 2/12 (2 months) old. The gravestone is barely legible but it appears their oldest son died as a child and is buried alongside William.

In 1849, German settlers built a frame grammar school next to the German Salem Lutheran Church on Ingleside Ave. This is where Henry Haug taught school in the 1860s.

Grandma was left with these two small boys, Edward and Henry. She married Albert Schmidt who had been a sea faring man. He was a very gentle man with a sort of limp in one leg. They came up north to Brooklyn, and bought a nice piece of property on Chauncey St. at the corner of Patchen Ave. He conducted a grocery store there and they raised three more children, Emma, Maggie and Albert, so there were five children in all.

LE: Eva Haug married Albert Schmidt on September 27, 1868, at the Evangelical Lutheran Church of St John in Brooklyn, New York. They bought the property at Chauncey St. and Patchen Ave. in August, 1875.

Edward (the oldest son) got married and had a job with the Prudential Insurance Company. At that time an agent called every week on those who had insurance. People generally paid 10 cents a week for they were middle-class people and salaries were small. Edward had one daughter, Elsie, and his wife's name was Anna, but she died at an early age. So Elsie was brought up by her Grandma and Grandpa Schmidt and the two maiden aunts, Emma and Maggie.

Henry married Henrietta Bermel who came from a family living on Chauncey St. up near Broadway. They were a big family and lived in a cobblestone house. Henry and Henrietta had five children: Eva, Henrietta, Eddie, Walter and Marguerite. Grandpa Carl Bermel was a tailor and sat with his legs folded under him at the table from what I heard. He too died at an early age. In fact, he died while his daughter Henrietta was carrying her first child, and that was me.

LE: Henry Haug and Henrietta Bermel were married October 12, 1884. Eva was born July 30, 1885 and named after her grandmother, Eva (Leonhauser) (Haug) Schmidt Henrietta's father, Carl Bermel died June 5, 1885, when he was 53 years old.

Grandma and Grandpa Schmidt did very well with the grocery store. It was a big one on the corner with large windows on both sides of the corner. They kept it immaculate. It had bare white wooden floors with sand from the seashore to keep it that way. They had a large dining room in the rear of the store, on the Patchen Ave. side, and a long narrow kitchen on the other side. It was a nice home with a parlor, back parlor and bedrooms upstairs and the top floor was rented out to a widow and her daughter. Grandma helped in the grocery store, Emmy went out as a sewing machine operator and Maggie stayed home, took care of the house and did all the housework and cooking. Albert married Margaret Hanlon and they had one daughter, Alberta.

FULTON STREET

In the meantime, my father, Henry, who was an out-of-doors type, bought an express wagon and a horse and went into the express business. This was in 1882 just a

Eva, born July 30, 1885

hundred years ago. My mother, Henrietta, rented a building at 1850 Fulton St. near Patchen Ave. She conducted a small store there, a miscellaneous store that sold candy, buns and rolls, tobacco, school supplies and toys, and even ice cream in the summertime, for then you could only buy ice cream in the winter. She was a very industrious type, opened the store at six o'clock and closed at eleven. We had a kitchen behind the store and upstairs we had three bedrooms and a living room and in later years a square piano.

Fulton Street showing the elevated railroad that ran past the Haug home and storefront.

I was born on Chauncey St. and my four brothers and sisters were born at 1850 Fulton St. At that time, there was no such thing as going to a hospital, babies were born at home. My father's express business grew and he soon had more horses, wagons and help. Grandma and Grandpa Schmidt had a stable built for him on Patchen Ave. right in the rear of their home. Dad had open trucks and horses, and made the trip to New York every day. He worked hard, never sat down before nine at night, and would fall asleep at the table. By the time he got home, the four of us, Henrietta, Eddie, Walter and I, would be upstairs asleep. But Marguerite, the baby of the family, was allowed to stay up to be with our Dad. She would stand on the back of his chair and comb his hair.

We all grew up and had busy lives. We all went to Public School 70 and had to walk about five blocks, going past Dad's stable and Grandma's grocery store, for the school was also on Patchen Ave. On his way home from school, my brother Eddie would deliver grocery orders for Grandpa Schmidt at his corner grocery store which we had to pass every day to and from school.

LE: P.S. 70 was on Patchen Ave. (between Macon and McDonough streets) and at least two of Eva's siblings did graduate from that school. But an entry in The Brooklyn Citizen newspaper, February 3, 1900, lists Eva Haug as having attended P.S. 35 and exempt from a graduation exam. P.S.35 (on Decatur St. and Lewis Ave.) was also about five blocks from the family home.

Our childhood was a very happy one. We had an exciting life on Fulton Street, the main shopping area. We all got along well and never had any arguments. My dad kept the boys busy after school hours, and Mother kept us girls busy washing the dishes, making the beds and assisting at whatever we could and minding the baby, Marguerite. We used to take her out in the baby carriage and ride around the block, for that block on Herkimer St. was all trees. As soon as I could see over the counter I helped in the store waiting on children wanting to buy candy.

We all went to Sunday school at the Reformed German Church on Herkimer St. near Howard Ave. We had to walk about a mile and we each got two cents to put in the collection plate. This was the same church that our mother and her family attended, at that time called "the white church on the hill." Her brothers and sisters all went to that church years before. We five were christened, confirmed and attended this church. We joined the choir and went back to Sunday school as teachers for our Uncle Ed eventually became superintendent.

When we got the measles or any of the children's sicknesses, my mother would get a mattress and put it on the kitchen floor and we all had to be sick together. Taking care of five children and waiting on the store was some job. When it came to Saturday and time to take a bath, Mother would put a large wooden tub on the kitchen floor and we took turns getting our baths. This large tub is the same one that she washed our clothes in and she would boil them on the stove in a large tin clothes boiler. How different today.

Eddie and Walter were always kept busy after school. The stable had six stalls. Father paid his mother $10.00 a month rent and the stable had a driveway next to it where he kept his express wagons. He had the boys take care of the bedding for the horses, and pay the feed bill and horse shoer every week. Eddie and Walter were never any bother to the family, they never smoked or went around with other boys.

BROOKLYN EAGLE POST CARD, SERIES 56, No. 336.
GERMAN REFORMED CHURCH, HERKIMER STREET
NEAR RALPH AVENUE.

My brothers went along with Dad as helpers and we never saw them except at mealtimes. When we all went to Sunday school, the boys and Dad had to feed the horses at noon and at night. The boys never had time to get into much trouble. Once Walter climbed into a tree across the street, and got up so high we had to get help to get him down and Mother punished him for that. Another time the boys were shooting craps across the street. A cop came and they all ran. Eddie was just a bystander and not one of the group, but the cop brought him home and he never did that again. They never went in for sports.

Edward, Eva, Henrietta, Walter and Marguerite (from left to right)

When we got older, we all had roller skates. And when the first street was cemented which was Decatur Street, it became a regular skating rink. We had a small pond at the corner of Fulton and Buffalo that we used to ice skate on, and at the corner of Patchen Ave. and Fulton there was a big deep lot we used for our sleighs belly-wopping.

I was named after our grandmother Eva Schmidt, being the first child, so every birthday she would buy me a pair of good shoes for children (Cox's). At Christmas, my mother's brother, Charlie Bermel, and his wife, would come down to visit us with big gifts such as wagons and sleighs for the boys and dolls and sewing baskets for the girls. We had a big phonograph with a large horn that played records and we would play it in the kitchen in the rear of the store. Mother let us have the neighbor children in and Father always came home late so it was alright.

We had a wonderful maiden lady who came in every week to clean upstairs, do the wash, and change the beds. On Saturdays, my sisters and I had to scrub the kitchen floor, clean the windows and clean the white marble mantle over the kitchen stove. We had gas light and heated our parlor upstairs with an oil heater and later a gas heater. Being on a business avenue, we were the first to have the electric light. We had no phones then or autos.

In the summer, Mother would have the cleaning girl, Carrie Schmidt, (no relation) mind the store and take us all out to Coney Island or Rockaway. She would take our neighbors, Mary and Henry, too. Mother would prepare a lunch and we would go bathing, romp on the beach and get home exhausted after supper.

The beach at Coney Island, circa 1904.

On Christmas Eve when Mother closed the store, Henrietta and I helped trim the Christmas tree in the parlor. Once in a while, Henrietta and I would take care of the store so that Mother could go to the theatre with some of the neighbors because they received free passes for having billboards in their store windows. She saw Lillian Russell, Ted Mack, and all the best of them. Dad would be home by nine so she did not worry about us.

We had a very good, generous mother. She never spoke badly of anyone. When Grandma Schmidt fell and broke her hip and was failing, she sent for my mother. Grandpa Schmidt and my father had already died and the two aunts had their mother make out a will. I don't know what she left Uncle Ed but she left us kids $10 each. I felt hurt but my brother, Eddie, said he had a good time with it. However, we all loved our grandma.

LE: Grandma Eva Schmidt died June 3, 1915, at the age of 79. In a codicil to her will, she added a distribution of $10 to six of her grand-children (about $266 in 2021 dollars).

Family photo for the 1906 wedding. Standing from left to right: Henrietta, Edward, Walter, Eva. Sitting: Henry, Marguerite, Henrietta

One Sunday our dad took us on a picnic with the horse and wagon. We drove out beyond Jamaica to Hollis Woods which was the end of town and had a toll gate. That was a long trip for a horse. I could go on, but want to say the most important thing in our young lives was when my mother's brother, Joseph, was Power President. This was around 1900 and his daughter, who was about the same age as me, was married. They had a wedding in the church by card invitation only, and a catered dinner at Uncle Joe's home which was a big one on Metropolitan Ave. We all got new dresses for the occasion and my dad had to hire one of those closed funeral coaches to get us over there. That was the only way one could travel then, either by coach or buggy. We had a family picture taken at the time and we still have the picture.

LE: The 1906 wedding of Eva's cousin, Eva Bermel to Henry Althoff, was a grand affair. The bride's father was Joseph Bermel (brother of Henrietta Haug) who had just been elected Borough president of Queens.

When Eddie graduated from grammar school, he went to work driving a horse and wagon for a baker. This was the same baker who supplied Mother with rolls and buns for her store every morning. Since Ed had to get up at 2:00 AM, he took a room nearby for $2.00 a week. He was only home on Saturdays and on Sundays he went out with a friend.

But Ed did not do this for long because Dad had a chance to buy out the business of another expressman, a Mr. Seiler. By that time, Dad had four horses and two extra express wagons, so he said Eddie was working so hard for this baker that he might as well work for him. So with Eddie working for Father, things were easier for Dad. He had faithful men working for him, one called Nolan and another older man that stuck with him all through the

Uncle Edward Haug

years. Before this, Dad would come home every night, cold and tired. He would have supper late and alone with Mother and baby Marguerite.

As an insurance collector, Uncle Ed was always dressed up. When he finished his route, he would come in almost every day, sit in the kitchen in the back of our store, play solitaire and have a meal. He had a furnished room around the corner at Lubeck's.

Later on Uncle Ed became superintendent of the Sunday school and he did a good job of it. We had over 200 attendees and he got Walter, who was married by that time, to become his assistant. I attended Sunday school until I was confirmed. Then Uncle Ed got me to take a class and I taught for 20 years and still keep up correspondence with one of my students who lives in California.

People used oil lamps at that time but we were lucky, being on the main avenue and in a business section, we had gas. We used Mantles and they gave a bright light. In the bedrooms we had a metal disc over the gas light, which over the open flame gave us heat.

LE: In the early 1900s, most working class households used oil lamps or candles for lighting. Gas lighting was considered modern and state-of-the-art at the time. Invented in 1890, a "mantle" was heated by a gas flame which then glowed brightly and lit up the room.

Mother bought a new cabinet Edison phonograph and then she got a square piano. The square piano gave us a lot of pleasure. Henrietta was very good at the piano and she took lessons. We all sang because she got all the latest songs. Henrietta would play steady from one song to the next. At night we would all be asleep before she finished. This made for lots of company for us girls but the boys never joined in.

When we had horse cars, I remember the first strike. Everyone kept indoors and the mounted police came up on the sidewalk. As children, we thought they would come in through the plate glass window. Talking about the plate glass window, when Walter was small, he got up early on a Sunday morning, climbed into the window, sat on a glass cake dish and ate all the charlotte-ruses while a crowd gathered outside. Otherwise, we were good kids.

The Great Trolley Strike by artist Frederick Remington at the National Postal Museum

LE: The strike was referred to as "The Great Trolley Strike of 1895." Eva was 9 ½ years old.

After the horse cars came the electric trolleys. The elevated trains would pass our window, but we were used to the noise and it did not bother us. But when we moved to Marion Street,

we could not sleep. It was too quiet and the whistles from the boats and the nightlife kept us awake. The elevated trains were taken down about 1960. Subway trains then took over and the trolleys have all been replaced by buses. For transportation, the airplane can take you anyplace in the world. In fact, we have very large planes that can take you to London and back in one day.

We saw the horse car go, and the trolley come in, as well as the elevated train, gas, the electric light, the phone, the typewriter, the automobile and we also saw the streets cemented. We had a sewing machine, a phone, and we were the first in the family to have an auto. So I would say we had a very interesting life.

Mother sold fireworks and did very well. The last year we had the store we did exceptionally well, and she cleared $1000. When Dad took on the additional business of Seiler's, Mother gave up the store and we then had an opportunity to buy a house at 119 Marion Street.

MARION STREET

The family needed larger quarters so when Mother gave up the store, my parents bought a 2 ½ story house at 119 Marion Street. This was in 1907. The back of the house adjoined the driveway of Dad's stable at Patchen Ave. near Marion St. Several years later, as the express business expanded, Dad was able to take things a little easier.

By the time we left Fulton Street and moved to Marion Street, we were all grown up. It was then that Eddie left the baker and went to work for Dad who had acquired the additional business from Seiler. George Reinhardt and Allie Rhein also went to work for Dad so he had it easier then. It was the first time in his life that he could send the trucks off, have lunch at home, go to his office dressed up, and get the freight ready for the trucks to pick up.

Once we no longer had the store, Mother and Dad went to church every Sunday night. They joined the Men's Club and Ladies' Club and enjoyed it. In October, 1909, they celebrated their 25th wedding anniversary and it was a big affair with all the families attending. It was held at Lubeck's Hall on Fulton Street, corner of Buffalo, and the dinner was served downstairs. They received a lot of gifts; cut glass had just become popular and there were at least six large bowls. The Men's and Ladies' Societies presented them with a cut glass vase 16 inches high. There were also many silver pieces, a table service for 12 from Mom's brother Charlie and a large tray and five-piece tea set from her brother Joe. The glass vase and large silver tea set still adorn our home.

The silver wedding of Henry J. Haug and his wife Henrietta of 119 Marion street, was celebrated Tuesday night at Buffalo Hall, corner Fulton street and Buffalo avenue. The couple were married twenty-five years ago at the German Reformed Church on Herkimer street. The Rev. Eckard, the present pastor of that church performed a second marriage ceremony for the couple. Mr. and Mrs. Haug have five children Eva, Henrietta, Edward, Walter and Marguerite, who were present. Among the guests was Mrs. E. Schmidt, mother of Mrs. Haug. About fifty guests participated in the banquet.

Newspaper article from The Chat, October 16, 1909

Not long after, we five were married within five years and Uncle Joe presented each of us with a set of tableware and silver service for 12. I have mine for over 60 years and it is as good as new.

We were all active in church work and involved in everything. We all attended Sunday school, the choir, the young people's society and Anniversary Day Parades. In fact, Eva and Henrietta were in a large choir and years later so were Hattie, John and Evelyn Haug, as well as Marguerite and George Ewing. The choir members in the first group were all married and for many years, had get-togethers at their homes. Eddie was confirmed in the class with Henrietta Erhardt, the pastor's daughter. Our organist, William Enners was with the choir 40 years, and married Henrietta Erhardt. When we had the church remodeled, Mr. Humburger, then an elder in the church, donated the new organ at a cost of $3,000. He enjoyed our choir so much that every now and then he would provide us with a social after the rehearsal, serving coffee and cake.

Mr. Curth, also an elder, would treat us with a sleigh ride. The sleigh seated 40 and was drawn by four horses. He rented it out and the sleigh was filled with hay and blankets to keep us warm. It had sleigh bells and we sang and had a wonderful time in "the winter wonderland." We drove through Prospect Park, down Coney Island Driveway and stopped at an inn and had coffee and cake to warm us up.

LE: "The sleigh was as large as a moving van and could easily accommodate 15 couples (stting on a straw-colored floor covered with yellow horse blankets). What a time we had driving through Prospect Park and down to a roadhouse on Ocean Parkway." (The Brooklyn Daily Eagle, April 23, 1939).

Another time all the choir members walked up to Forrest Park after rehearsal to watch Haley's Comet although we never did see it. Our brothers were never in anything like this – they were much younger.

A 1905 bicycle advertisement

Our sister Henrietta was the only sport in the family. She was the only one who took piano lessons and the only one who had a bicycle.

LE: Bicycles, up until the 1890s, were almost exclusively for men. With the invention of a bicycle that was deemed safe and appropriate for women and children, women gained a means of exercise, as well as freedom of movement – and without a chaperone! The bicycle phenomenon also impacted fashion and helped women get out of those long, restrictive skirts.

Henrietta also went to Madam Schnurbush to take lessons in dressmaking. She had wonderful clothes and her hats were the latest, handmade by Mrs. Fisher (a tenant of Grandma's) who worked downtown in a large millinery salon. I worked every day from 8 AM to 6 PM. It was only years later that we had shorter hours and were off a 1/2 day on Saturday. We two sisters went everywhere together – at that time we had no boyfriends. We went to dancing school, the weekly Saturday night dances and the movies around the corner. We always had someplace to go in the evenings. Henrietta saw to it and she would make all the arrangements. On Sunday nights we liked to play cards and Mother and Father would join us. We also had a double set of dominoes, and though we had no autos at that time, we enjoyed ourselves.

Henrietta and I had wonderful times on Marion Street. We took in everything. On the open trolley car for five cents, we would go to Canarsie on Sunday. We visited an aunt there. And for many years there were two boys who used to come to see us and spend the day. We had autos by then. We took boat trips up the Hudson River to Kingston Point or to Bear Mountain or Poughkeepsie. We would go to Brighton Beach – they had a big hotel there and a boardwalk. We also took trips to Coney Island for five cents and went to Luna Park, Dreamland, and Feltmans. They all had bands and we were crazy about dancing. We even went to dancing schools on Saturday nights. We also took the sleeper train to Washington. We would leave Saturday night at 10:00, sleep in our seats and get to Washington at 5:00 AM. We would go to the Capitol and the Smithsonian Museum, leave at 4:00 and reach home before dark.

Luna Park, Coney Island, NY

Feltmans Restaurant, Coney Island, NY

Ball Room and Balcony, Dining Room, Stauch's, Coney Island, N. Y

Sometimes we took the Long Island Railroad and a boat to Block Island too. I worked for L. Curth & Sons and Mr. Curth and his daughter had a nice home there. I was always welcome to spend my vacation there for a week. After supper, everyone went down to the village to get the mail that generally came up from the city at 8:00. I had two boyfriends then and whichever one I met first, I would go out with for the evening. One had a carriage with wheels and one year I took Henrietta with me. Eugene said we will have to get someone for her, so who comes along

Stauch's Ballrooom, Coney Island

but Frank Wecht. Gene introduced her and she spent the evening with Frank, so Gene and I got rid of them. I had another boyfriend that played in the band and worked in the knife shop where Frank worked. I kept up correspondence with them for years. They even came down to visit us. However, I was not the marrying kind and not one for petting. But Frank and Henrietta became serious.

Excursion boat to Block Island

One year I went up to Ellenville with Otto Curth to surprise his dad. Cars were just coming in and he had a large one. Everything went alright until we reached Middletown. We had to cross over a high mountain along a narrow road. When we came down the other side it had rained hard and there were puddles everywhere. Otto drove through every puddle and laughed when we got splattered with mud and all over the new automobile dusters and caps too. Then the car stopped and we were stuck. We had another couple with us and the boys thought that mud must be clogging the motor. So they made trips to the farmhouse nearby and threw buckets of water over the motor. The bakery wagon from Ellenville came along and asked us if he could help but we were only about 20 miles from town and said no. But when the baker came back, we were tired and let him tow us back into town. We went the back way so we would not be seen, for all along the road folks would shout, "Get a horse." The next morning we intended to take the car in for repair, but to our surprise, the motor turned over and nothing was wrong. The motor had dried out overnight.

LE: Early driving was a chaotic and stressful experience! In the first 10 years of the 1900s, there were no stop signs, traffic lights, lane lines, brake lights, driver's licenses, posted speed limits, etc.

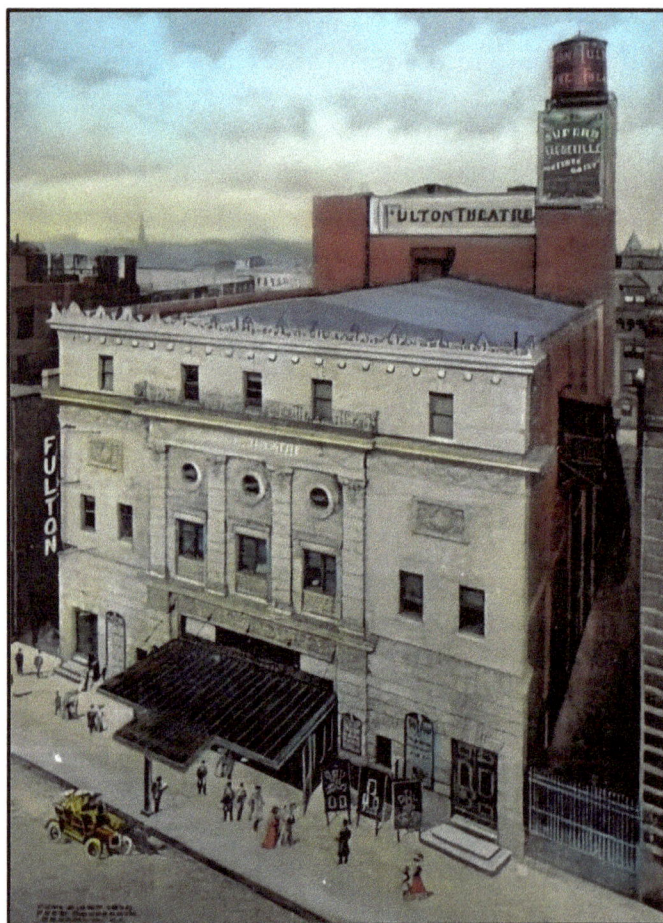

Fulton Street Theatre, Brooklyn

We went to the moving picture house on Sumpter Street around the corner every week and to dances every Saturday night. Henrietta was the sport in the family. She would plan these things and when I came home from work, she would have made plans for us.

I met Ted at a movie around the corner. It was crowded and we had to stand in the back until we could get seats. I had a little velvet hat on with a bird and a big long tail. Henrietta said that I was annoying the man behind me with the tail. He overheard us and said, "No, it is not annoying me." When seats were available, the usher (who knew us) brought this young man (Ted) and sat him alongside us. He must have bribed the usher.

Ted walked us home, just around the corner and when we got to the gate, Henrietta went in and left me with him. Ted thought I was Mr. Curth's daughter as he had seen Mr. Curth at my desk in the office as he passed by to get the elevated tram. I did not make a date with him but he phoned and took me to a vaudeville show, I think it was at the Fulton Theatre. It was a fine place but it was scary having mixed drinks which he ordered, and with him being so friendly with the waiters. Ted sensed it and reassured me so that I would be at ease. He appreciated being with a different sort of person than those he mixed with in New York. That's where he lived until his folks bought a house on Herkimer Street right in back of our house on Fulton Street. I never made a date but he would phone and ask if I would go to Trommers summer garden with him. Ted was so dressed up and attractive. I always told my family that I was going to shake him. They all thought he was a fast type.

MAPLE GARDEN — TROMMER'S BREWERY RESTAURANT — BROOKLYN, N. Y.   D-3004

Well, Ted went to Buffalo to take charge of a $1.00 shirt shop. And when Henrietta married Frank, Ted joined them at their hotel that night on their honeymoon. I put Ted out of my mind. But it was not long after that he phoned me from Grand Central saying he was finished in Buffalo and we went to Trommers for dinner. At that time, I was seeing Clarence Curth and whoever phoned first, I accepted. Then Ted had an interview with Thomas Edison at his Jersey plant. Edison hired him to introduce the new Edison cabinet and Ted toured the west giving performances at parent and civic meetings.

LE: An interesting side note about Ted. He was mentioned in The Indianapolis Star newspaper, (Oct 28, 1915) as having attended a Republican campaign meeting. "Speeches were also made by Edwin H. Lenning of the Edison Laboratory of West Orange, N.J."

By this time I had forgotten Ted when I got a wire to meet him at Grand Central. It was summer and I had been bathing at Coney Island which I often did in the morning. I had nothing else to do so I met him. I remember I was dressed all in white with a white coat, the latest at that time. He wore a checked black and white suit, and a straw hat and cane. He hailed one of those open cabs that you see in Central Park and when we reached a famed eating house, the doorman gave us special attention. He thought we were a bride and groom.

About this time, our Uncle Ed (Dad's brother) became Sunday school Superintendent. I was 18 and he asked me to teach a class of boys which I enjoyed. I had Charlie Miller, John Dinger, Fred Schultheiss and Bill Ahlrich, names you probably recognize. I taught them for about 10 years. They are all gone now except Bill Ahlrich, who has kept up correspondence with me all these years. Today he is 74 and I am 94. He is still in Covina, CA, in charge of a large newspaper as head of advertising.

Dad enjoyed these few years, business was good. He could go over to his office at 85 Reade St. in Manhattan after lunch and take care of the shoe market and have things ready for the trucks. But this was only for a few years until he developed gland trouble. He was then 49 and went to the hospital for an operation. His doctor guaranteed us that everything would be alright but he lived only a few days. Dad died in 1910.

Mother took Walter, then 17, from school to help Eddie who was 19 and well acquainted with the business. The boys had good competent help who had been with Dad for many years. Uncle Charlie Bermel, my mother's brother, called on the firms they did business with and offered bond for the two boys who were now going to run Haug's Express by themselves. Each and every firm stated they had full confidence and would continue to give the Haug boys their business.

The boys worked hard. They were well trained by our Dad and we all helped as best we could. Mother took orders and Henrietta did all the bookkeeping. There was always someone home to take phone calls. The boys carried on and business was very good. We all got along very well and never had any arguments.

All this time Eddie was seeing a floor lady (Louise) at the company where she worked and where Eddie stopped every day to pick up shipments. He married her in 1913 and Walter was best man. They lived next door to us in the flat and it was here that Henry, the first grandchild, was born in 1915.

Meanwhile, I was working at Curth's for $6.00 a week which was good pay at that time. Moving men, for example, were getting only $1.50 a day and it was not steady work. Earlier I had worked for a real estate office across the way for a year or so. I took typewriting and

Miner's Business Academy, Hancock St. and Patchen Ave., Brooklyn, N. Y.

shorthand at Minor's Business Academy at night. But the real estate office wanted me to work until 7:00 at night, so I left because I could not make it to the school in time. I was at the head of my class but did not finish because then I got the job at Curth & Sons; they needed a girl for the office. It was only a block away and I stayed there for 18 years until age 32 when I left to get married.

Louise and baby Henry spent a lot of time with us because Eddie was often late coming home. Her maiden name was Bachman and her father, mother, sister and brother lived in Ridgewood, Queens. They were a Catholic family. Our mother taught Louise how to crochet and she was always busy. Louise made a bedspread for every bed in her house, four or more. She went to the hospital to have the rest of her children.

In 1913, Mother took a trip to Germany and she took Marguerite along who was about 17 years old. They visited a sister of Grandpa Karl Bermel. Her married name was Altenkirch and her daughter Dietrich lived in Leipzig. They called Mother "Guldener Tante" meaning Golden Aunt because she took them out and paid the bills. While over there, Mother and Marguerite visited Frankfurt, Rudolstadt, Cologne, and Switzerland and were gone two months. Henrietta took care of the house and the two boys and myself.

LE: Rudolstadt, Germany is the town where Eva's grandfather, Karl Bermel, was born in August 1831.

The following year Mother put another floor on the house as well as a new square stoop. She made an apartment ready for Marguerite and George to move into in 1916 after they were married.

Henrietta married Frank Wecht in 1915. They had a big wedding at the Pouch Mansion with about 50 guests. I was the maid of honor and Marguerite was the bridesmaid. Henrietta and Frank went to Niagara Falls on their honeymoon. That's when Ted, who was manager of a $1.00 men's shirt shop, met them at their hotel.

Henrietta and Frank went to Port Jervis to live and Frank went into the wet wash business with his brother, Jake. However, they did not get along very well. When Eddie and Walter heard of an expressman who wanted to go out of business in Ridgewood, Henrietta and Frank bought the business and have lived in Ridgewood, Queens ever since.

Built in 1887, the Pouch Mansion became the most popular venue in Brooklyn for weddings and balls, and political and religious meetings.

We settled Dad's estate when Marguerite was 21 years old. My mother owned the house at 119 Marion St. She gave each of us girls $300 and the boys received the Express business.

LE: This occurred April 26th, 1917. In a legal Bill of Sale, Henrietta sold Haug's Express to her two sons for one dollar and the three sisters signed off on the document.

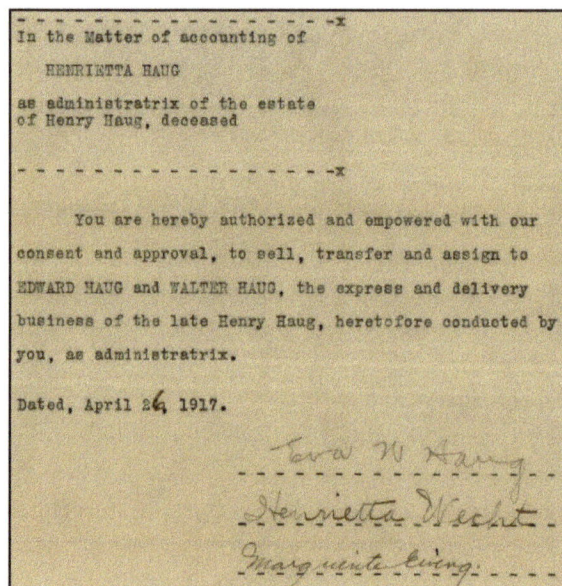

By that time my brothers and sisters were all married. In a double church wedding in 1916, Walter married Hattie Reinhardt and Marguerite married George Ewing. Walter and Hattie had an apartment near Sumner Avenue. George and Marguerite moved into the second floor of 119 Marion St. and Mother and I lived on the top nearly finished floor.

TWO COUPLES WED AT ONCE.

Miss Reinhardt to Mr. Haug, Miss Haug to Mr. Ewing.

Brooklyn Times Union, June 14, 1916

In 1917, I bought a Ford car, the first in the family. It was a Ford because Otto Curth (the youngest of L. Curth & Sons) was given the Ford Agency. I was able to get one for less than $500. My 1917 Ford touring car cost $360, less 10% which came to $324.00.

TELEPHONE
7405 BEDFORD

SERVICE STATION
244-250 MARION ST.

BROOKLYN, N.Y. June 21st, 1917 191

M iss Eva Haug. #720 Herkimer St. Brooklyn. N. Y.

Ford
THE UNIVERSAL CAR

CURTH AUTO SALES CO.

33-35 SUMPTER STREET

COR. PATCHEN AVE.

TERMS:

1	Touring Car (Ford) # 1971293	$ 360. 00	
	Less 10%	36. 00	
			$ 324. 00
	Freight		18. 40
	Tire Holder		1. 50
	Speedometer (Dash)		8. 00
	Demountables		30. 00
	Amount		$ 381. 90
	Deposit		50. 00
			$ 331. 90

1st car

With the new car, Eddie and Walter each took a day off to take their family, as well as Mother, to the beach. All their children were small. I worked at Curth's until 1918 when I left to get married.

This is most likely Eva's Ford. Photo taken around 1919 in front of the Wecht home at Port Jervis, NY. Standing far left is Henrietta (Eva's mother). Brother Ed is at the wheel with his wife Louise sitting on the running board. Their son Gene is in the front seat, Edward is standing on the running board and Henry is above the wheel. Frank Wecht is in the back seat.

I was starting to keep company with Ted and when I got that car, he was around every night. Mother was always ready to go riding too. I never had a chance to drive. Ted was always on the job and he had to take one night off a week to rest up.

That summer we took Mother along on my vacation. We drove up to Springfield, Massachusetts to visit Ted's uncle, Doctor Tracy. Then we drove on through Rhode Island, Vermont and Maine, through the White Mountains, back through Rutland, Vermont, crossed the Lake to the other side and made Ellenville on the way back. He had some nerve but Mother and I enjoyed it.

By that time, Mother and I were living alone at Herkimer Street. All the rest had married and Mother went out with us on all the trips. Then came the war. Ted had served 10 years with the 71st Regiment in New York and was afraid of being called. So he asked me to marry him in front of Mother and I said I was not ready.

Well, he took a job as a private chauffeur for chauffeurs were exempt from serving in the military. His employer told Ted she had a summer home at Keene Valley. She wanted to leave the first week in May and would be away all summer. She asked if Ted was married and he said yes. So they readied an apartment for us over their big garage with an entrance on the rear street. She lived on Montague St., a very wealthy neighborhood in downtown Brooklyn and had a Rolls-Royce car. She fitted him out with a uniform. So we had to go through with getting married.

Photo circa 1925. Eva is in the center. Her sister Henrietta Wecht is above her, with nieces Marion Haug (left) and Ruth Haug (right).

We were married on April 30, 1918, by Judge Fawcett who was a Supreme Court judge I had known when he was a young lawyer. We had to do this because Ted was Catholic. I did not know what day it would be, but when the judge called and said he could marry us that afternoon, I phoned Mother and the girls. I left the office by noon, met Ted and we were married that afternoon. When we arrived home, the family had gathered, the girls had baked cakes and the eats were furnished by Henry Day. It was a beautiful day and a fine time for us.

The armistice came and by that time Ted's employer had found out that Ted was no mechanic. So we moved into the top floor of Walter's house and lived there for many years. Ted's parents lived on the next block at 841 Herkimer Street.

BALTIMORE COUSINS

We had an Aunt Lena in Baltimore who was a cousin of my father's. She married a man named Fink and had a grocery store. They had three boys, Phil, Fred and George and a daughter, Katherine.

Phil worked at the B&O Railroad and was married but had no children. Fred never married and owned one of the largest drug stores in the heart of Baltimore next to the B&O building. He took his brother, George, into the business with him. He was not married either. Aunt Lena's daughter was married and she had one daughter named Doris. They visited us often and we, in turn, visited them. We had a lot of enjoyment showing them New York and Coney Island.

When Eddie and Louise were married, they spent their honeymoon at Aunt Lena's home in Baltimore and when her daughter Katherine married, she and her husband came up to our

A young Ed Haug. Photo probably taken on Marion St. outside the family home.

house on their honeymoon. Katherine was married only a few years when her husband died (in the 1918 flu epidemic) and left her with the baby girl, Doris. Then she went back to live with her father and mother.

The drug store was a gold mine and the boys became wealthy. They bought their mother a large house after their father died. They had a happy time for some years but then one after the other died and all their wealth went to Katherine and her daughter Doris.

Doris married, had no children and when her mother died she inherited everything. They still live on the outskirts of Baltimore, spend the winters in Florida and take all kinds of cruises around the world.

HERKIMER STREET

The home at 119 Marion Street was my mother's and after we settled my father's estate, Eddie and Walter became co-owners of the express business.

In February, 1920, the boys bought two attached 2½ story houses with a two-story brick building 25' x 100'. This building had a basement which had been equipped to hold 40 horses. Mr. Culliford, the owner, had had a livery business there and wanted to retire. It was well suited for the boys. Eddie lived in one house and Walter in the other. Walter had previously been renting 720 Herkimer St. and Evelyn was the first child to be born there. In the years after, all the children were born there, went to school and married while they lived at 718 and 720 Herkimer St. The business grew larger all the time and so did the families. By 1921, the boys had converted the business from horses to auto cars which made things easier.

I was only married one year when WW I ended and the Armistice was signed in 1919. We moved back into the top floor of 720 Herkimer St. for Walter was already in the lower part. Then Eddie and his family moved to 718 Herkimer and the express business moved also. We had many pleasant years together. Henry was a baby when Eddie moved in but the rest of his children were all born there.

After the business moved to Herkimer St., along with Eddie, Walter, Henrietta and me, Mother was left living alone on the top floor of 119 Marion St. with Marguerite on the second floor. Not long after, Mother acted as a bridesmaid to a friend and met Karl Koenig and they married. Karl was a bachelor who just came in and hung up his hat. He resigned from being an insurance agent for the Prudential Insurance Company where he could have

Henrietta and Charles Koenig outside their home at Lake Ronkonkoma

received a pension in two more years. They were married in June 1923. He was good to her and they were very happy.

About two years later, Mother and Karl saw a house they liked, so they moved to their new home at Lake Ronkonkoma. It was a corner house on the main road around the Lake and their neighbor was Fiedler. They were very happy there and Eddie at that time had his house on the main road on the other side of the Lake. Haug's Express took over Mother's house at 119 Marion St. and paid her for it. However, Eddie and Walter had trouble with tenants and eventually sold it.

LAKE RONKONKOMA

In 1924, my brother Edward, and his family, along with Henrietta and Frank Wecht, visited Mr. Decker who operated the Lake Front Hotel in Lake Ronkonkoma, Long Island. The family liked the location so much and the beach with white sand that they spent the summer there. My brother, Walter and his family, also spent their vacation there.

The Lake Front Hotel was on a large piece of property. And next door was a large vacant house with six bedrooms called "The Casino." Edward rented the Casino the following year with the option to buy. He bought it the following year and when the deal was closed, Ed gave Paula Brown (the real estate woman), part of the land which was to be his in exchange for seven lots around the corner. She wished to develop the section and cut it up into streets.

Eva and Ted Lenning's bungalow at Lake Ronkonkoma

Sunny Road, Lincoln Road, Harding Road and the road in front of the seven lots were deeded to Edward and it was named Haug Road. This road was only 200 feet long and beyond that it was white sand. Paula Brown specified that it could not be used commercially, but a few years later she turned the house next door into a tavern and it was operated many years later by Jack Brown.

After the streets were cut through, Paula Brown built a number of houses on Lincoln Road and she occupied the one on the corner of Sunny Road. She continued selling the houses or selling the lots and had them built for others. The Lake Front Hotel was very large and not doing well so she sold it to Capt. Rorick. The hotel was originally set back from the road. She moved it further forward and afterward, it burnt down.

My brother, Edward, built a bungalow on the rear lots and rented it out for the summer. The Enders family rented it one summer. But it was a nuisance to the family, so I bought the bungalow from him, along with three additional lots making my property five lots. All the other sections were wild.

FAMILY LIFE

By 1925, my sister, Marguerite and her husband George, moved to Tarrytown. George worked at the Kelvinator Refrigerator Company. It was there that Marguerite had a nervous breakdown and her mind never completely recovered.

My two brothers were so different. Eddie was involved in social and civic activities and Walter enjoyed church, baseball, handball and the beach. Eddie's children were involved in

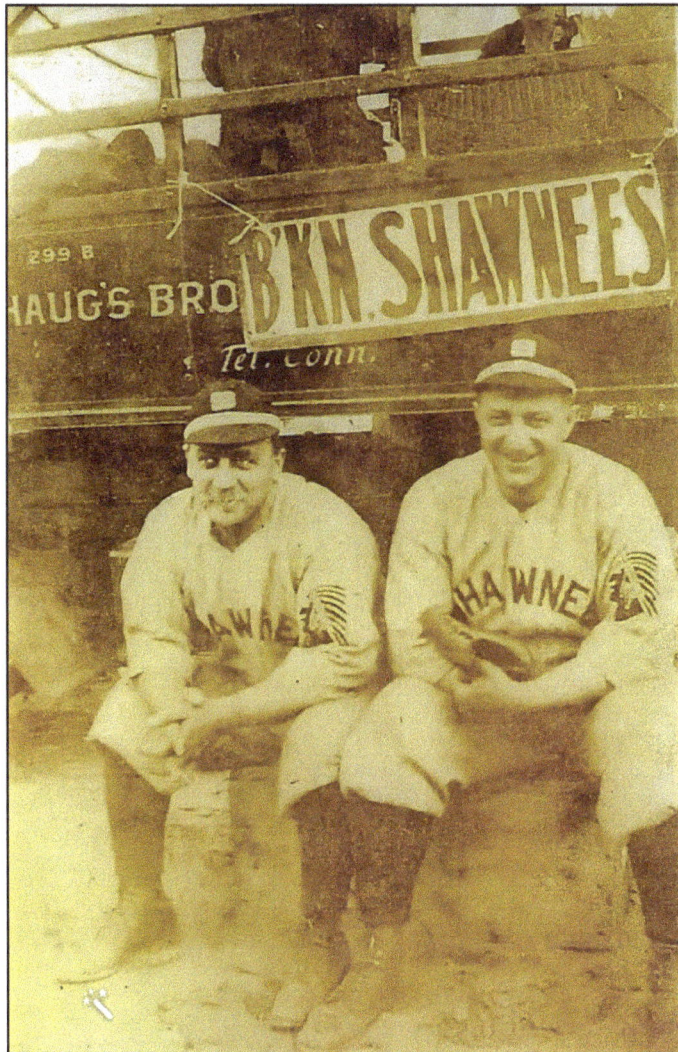

Walter Haug (left). Unidentified man on the right. Baseball team sponsored by Haug's Express

mechanical work and education and took no interest in sports or music, not even the billiard table in the basement.

Both wives, Louise and Hattie, were wonderful housewives and mothers. They lived separate lives and never quarreled about anything. Their boys were always there to help both their dads unload and reload trucks and acted as tailboys whenever they could. Despite all the children, Louise and Hattie's homes were immaculate, you never saw books or clothes scattered around. In fact, Hattie painted her kitchen and had new oil cloth for the kitchen every year, and fresh kitchen curtains every two weeks.

As the business grew, Haug's Express needed more help and Hattie's brothers, George, Willie, Paul, and Allie Rhein (her sister's husband) worked there too. They lived a few doors away.

Eddie and Walter also branched out. They bought places at the beach for their summer homes, Eddie at Lake Ronkonkoma and Walter at Roxbury. They both had cars. Eddie's children were Henry, Edward, Eugene, Marion and Ruth. Walter had John, Evelyn, and Helen.

At Christmas we assembled together and had a real live Santa Claus. Every year we had to choose another person to play the part so the children would not know who it was. This custom was carried on and still is for the past 50 years or more.

Walter was interested in the church and so was I, while Henrietta and Eddie led more social lives. When our Uncle Ed was superintendent of the Sunday school, Walter was the assistant. I was in the choir for many years and taught a class in Sunday school for about 20 years. Many of our family members were in the choir from time to time. The children all went to church every Sunday too, we packed the car.

The boys became Masons and Eddie was very active. In 1922 they organized the Square Club in the church basement of the Reformed Church. All our families, friends, and members of the church joined and it flourished all these years. Until this year, 1979, Edward Haug and George Ewing were the remaining charter members. But now that Edward has died, George is the remaining charter member for over 50 years.

1933 - Standing left to right: Frank Wecht, Henrietta Wecht, Ed Haug, Louise Haug, Ted Lenning, Charles Koeing. Seated: Eva Lenning, Hattie Haug, Grandma Henrietta (Haug) Koenig, Walter Haug, Marguerite Ewing

1945 - Standing left to right: Ted Lenning, Ed Haug, Walter Haug, George Ewing, Frank Wecht. Seated: Eva Lenning, Louise Haug, Hattie Haug, Marguerite Ewing, Henrietta Wecht, Grace Ewing

In 1929, Walter became interested in starting a Boy's Brigade for the Sunday school. So he borrowed $1000 from our mother and equipped a group of young boys in Sunday school with uniforms. A friend of the family, Henry Keil, who had much experience with the 13th Regiment, drilled the boys and the unit made a wonderful showing at our Sunday School Anniversary in June. It eventually disbanded when the Boy Scouts came in, but our Sunday school was always the best and the biggest.

So here ends the story of Henry Haug, to be taken up by future lives and a new generation.

———————————

Eva and Ted Lenning, July 1945

October 1956 - Henrietta Wecht, Edward Haug, Eva Lenning, Frank Wecht

July 1970 - The 3 sisters: Eva Lenning, Henrietta Wecht, Marguerite Ewing

LE: As I mentioned at the beginning, Aunt Eva did a wonderful job writing memories of her family and growing up in Brooklyn. For the Haug family descendants, how fortunate we are to have her recollections and this glimpse of life in a bygone era.

In November, 1963, Aunt Eva was honored with a testimonial dinner and reception for having taught Sunday school for over 30 years. As described in a lengthy newspaper article in the Kings County Chronicle, about 100 people attended, including family and many of her former students. The ceremony opened with a prayer and a toast in her honor followed by the reading of telegrams of congratulations. Then several nieces and nephews shared their memories of Aunt Eva and Uncle Ted. Here are just a few:

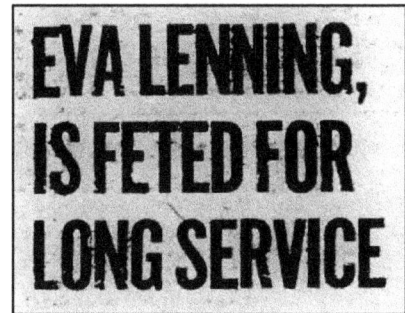

> **John Haug**: *If ever I got the urge to run away from home, all I had to do was go up a flight of stairs – how comforting. Uncle Ted was there with the eternal pipe in his easy chair in a softly lit room reading the newspaper and listening to the new-fangled radio – peaceful. Aunt Eva would be in the living room, somehow having a kinship to the bust of Marie Antoinette sitting alongside of her, as she went through the hair-combing ritual – fascinating.*

> *Aunt Eva's closet always seemed so much bigger that it actually was! Always crammed with presents for everyone bought a year or more ahead. It was opened with great secrecy when we were there and little was revealed. Still it was fun to try and figure out what I might get when my turn came – very interesting.*

> *I remember Uncle Ted puttering around his taxi – the shiniest one in town. And the day I got caught nipping in the wine decanter in their refrigerator – how embarrassing!*

> *As a young boy, I remember these BIG cars driving up to the curb at Herkimer St. Uncle Ted, the chauffeur, would get out of the car, smoking his pipe and dressed to perfection. He would let me look inside the car because it had gold handles.*

> *I remember everyone had to take turns listening to the radio in those days – BUT if you went upstairs to the Lenning's, they had a radio set with THREE sets of earphones, so that three of us could listen at once. When our mother was looking for us, she would find us up at Aunt Eva's and Uncle Ted's with ears glued to the radio.*

1935 - Grandma and Grandpa William Lenning

Uncle Ted, being a private chauffeur, liked big cars – so naturally his own car was BIG too. One day Grandpa Lenning decided to buy a car and drive. He went to the local Ford dealer and purchased a new Model-A Ford car. Grandpa Lenning never did learn to drive so Uncle Ted had to drive around in this little Ford – and came to like little cars too.

In more recent years, most of the activity centered round Lake Ronkonkoma. We all got together and painted the house in one day – but we left the windows for Uncle Ted.

We all spent some time at the roadside stand, Haug's Casino. Everyone helped – waiting on customers, washing dishes and of course hanging around meeting all your friends and relatives.

__Helen (Haug) DeArellano__: In the bathroom of 720 Herkimer Street, a big event was happening – Aunt Eva was getting ready to get her hair shampooed. I don't remember the hair dresser's name, but she would pull up a stool for me to sit on and watch – for when Aunt Eva let down her long hair, it almost reached to the bottom of the tub.

There are many other memories: I remember the Happy Easter parties we had at Aunt Eva's with the brown clay bunnies that held jelly beans. When Easter Sunday came along, Aunt Eva would have the largest corsage in the entire congregation. It was easy to sing along with Aunt Eva sitting next to you in the pew because she carried the alto part real strong.

I remember Uncle Ted and his early morning coughing – and in a deep voice he would say, "How long are you going to be in that bathroom?" Sometimes we would visit Grandma and Grandpa Lenning up the street and Grandpa would have a pipe in his hand, just like Uncle Ted.

Then on special occasions, we would visit Aunt Eva and Uncle Ted at the Lake and take a swim with Aunt Eva joining in. Afterward, she would take our pictures. In the early evening, Aunt Eva would come down to the stand and buy us all ice cream. Then we would all go back to their house and sit on the front porch and look at the many photos in the picture album which they had taken many years ago.

Eva (left) and her sister Henrietta at Haug's Casino, Lake Ronkonkoma, circa 1930. The child in the water is their niece, Marion Haug (my mother)..

I remember all the Easters, Christmases and Birthdays – and how they remembered us all – wrapping all those gifts and walking to the post office to see that they were sent off on time.

Henry Haug: *Around 1931, Aunt Eva and Uncle Ted used to take me along on weekends when they were going to their place at the Lake. The 1931 Ford they had was new and fast. Often times when we stopped for a traffic light on the Jericho Turnpike, a bigger and more powerful car would be alongside us. When the light changed to green and if Uncle Ted was in the mood, we would take off smooth and fast. Uncle Ted would shift gears as though he was in no hurry – BUT I remember smiling many times when he did this because one thing gave him away. The pipe that usually hung down from his mouth would be standing straight out!*

Eva and Ted's 50th anniversary, April 1968

In September, 1970, Eva's husband, Ted, died at the age of 85. They had been married over 52 years.

Eva went on to live another 14 years and she continued to be very active. She was so very proud of all her nieces and nephews and their extended families and she did an amazing job corresponding with a wide circle of family and friends. Even at the age of 96, she was still typing letters, with the help of a large print typewriter that she just loved. Here is part of one of her letters after a visit to one of her nieces (March 26, 1981):

Dear Marion & George,

We made it home in good time and it was still daylight at 6:15. . . .I enjoyed seeing your home so much and all the antiques of the years gone by, my mother's dinner set, Mother Lenning's and my sets from the Lake. I have been in a daze all morning thinking about them and how wonderful you kept everything and if I don't get down there again, the memory will stay with me.

I also enjoyed the wonderful dinner. I had the turkey and stuffing for lunch and have enough for another lunch tomorrow.

We talked all the way home and I fell asleep listening to the news. I was so tired out. I am very happy I was able to make the trip.

Wish both of you good health and contentment and happiness and May God bless you and watch over you and Louise and Georgie too. With Love, Aunt Eva at 96.

Eva was always close to her brother, Eddie, and after her husband died, the two of them would get together once a week. They enjoyed reminiscing. They also went for acupuncture treatments together. And at the age of 91 Eva experienced her very first airplane flight when she and Eddie flew to Sarasota, Florida.

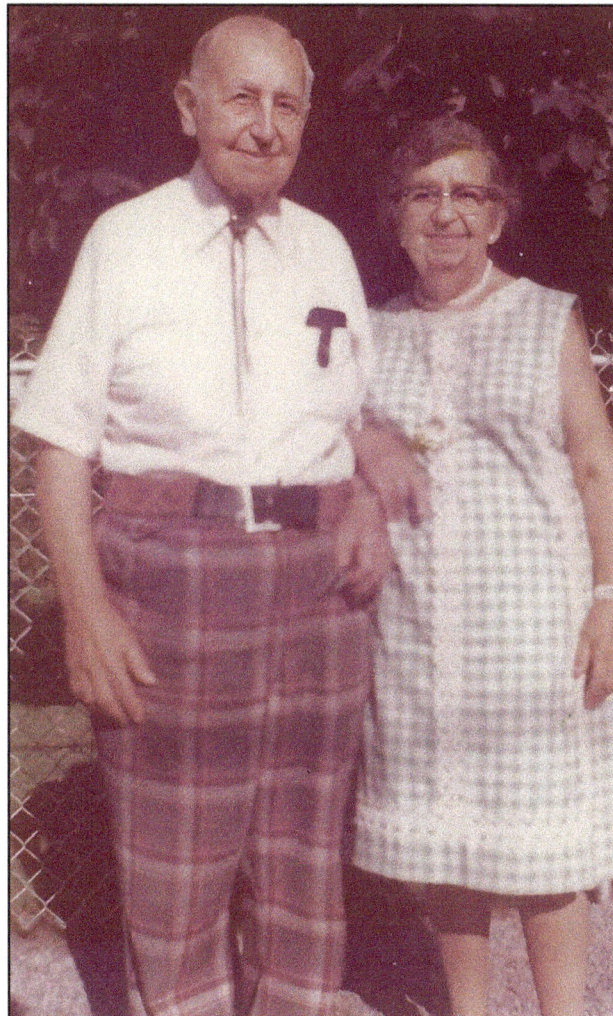

Here is an excerpt from another one of her letters to her brother (August 16th, 1977):

Dear Eddie,

You can't appreciate how happy you made me with the surprise party for my birthday and I don't know how to begin to thank you and also Edward and Virginia for the work they put into it.

The words, "thank you," are insufficient for an affair such as we had, the memory of it will always be with me. . . . We are all in good health and we had a happy time, and at this time of life, truly we all are very blessed and I know you and I are so very thankful to be in gatherings of this kind.

I also prized all the greeting cards, I received 30 of them.

It is at this time I am reminded that it has been seven years since Ted has left us, and Eddie you will really never know how much your weekly visits meant to me all these years. . . your advice and suggestions.

We are not a family to speak of our feelings but deep down in our hearts our love is there and when we are needed we are on hand to help. You can be <u>very</u> proud of all your children, every one of them is so concerned about you and will go to no length to give you pleasure. Your advice and influence in my life has made it possible for me to carry on as I have and I will always feel indebted to you for your advice and understanding.

I must say the many hours we spent going down "Memory Lane" I enjoyed and made me appreciate the fact that we are still here and in good health to enjoy our lives. While I miss the day a week for the past seven years, I will close with a verse from the Bible, "The Lord watch between me and thee, when we are absent one from another." (Genesis 31:49)

With all my love and the hope that God will bless you with continued good health and watch over you

Lovingly, Your Sister,

Eva

July 1983 - Eva's 98th birthday at the home of Eugene Haug in Floral Park, NY

When my brother, George, was teaching near Aunt Eva's home in Queens, she took such an interest in his students. She even saved materials for their arts and crafts projects. She wrote a lengthy letter to George describing how he was following in the footsteps of her grandfather who had also been a school teacher and conducted the church choir. From just a few lines of her letter you can feel and hear her excitement. She was 90 years old when she typed this letter:

Dear George,

I was so enthused after your phone call the other night telling me of your interest in a group of boys singing and composing music and having fun doing it. I was so excited I could not go to sleep for you are following in my Grandpa Henry Haug's footsteps. And I want to encourage you and give you some good advice when you have time to talk to me again on the phone.

Aunt Eva also sent me many kind and encouraging cards and letters while I was in the military. And even in her mid-90s, she kept up with current events. Here are a few examples from her letters to me:

August 11, 1980 – Everything here this week is Convention. The Democratic Convention is being held at Madison Square Garden here in New York. President Carter is trying for a second term and Kennedy is running against him. On the other side, the Republicans have chosen Ronald Reagan from California. Years ago he was an actor and several years ago he was Governor of California and the big excitement will come in November on Election Day, the first Tuesday in November. (Aunt Eva at 95)

February 8, 1981 – We have just gotten over ten days of excitement, the Inauguration. That was followed by the Hostages, their landing in Germany, then at West Point and finally their arrival in New York, where they sure did have some Welcome Home Party.

Letters to her great-niece Louise Eckhardt

Their dinner at Waldorf-Astoria, then the Ticker Tape Parade and finally the Christmas dinner at Luchow's where they had a large XMAS tree decorated with large yellow ribbons, a sight they will always remember. I forgot the welcome on the lawn at the White House. The weather was real mild, the men without overcoats. But for the Ticker Tape parade, the weather had changed that morning and it was very cold and very windy, but nothing could keep the crowd back. (Aunt Eva at 96)

April 15, 1981 – I was at the TV three hours and missed nothing of the space ship's countdown and have a good idea of the desert and the base. It sure was thrilling and it must have been more so for you. (Aunt Eva at 96)

As evidenced by these few sample letters, Aunt Eva was extremely interested in the news of the day and took great delight in everything!

On January 4, 1984, Eva Lenning passed away peacefully in her home at the age of 98. In her will she bequeathed $1,000 to George Ewing, the husband of her sister – as well as $1,000 to each spouse of her nieces and nephews – 10 in all. The remainder of her estate she left in equal shares to her 10 nieces and nephews.

Eva Lenning was a remarkable person! She was incredibly proud of her family and always interested, always encouraging, always supportive to those in her large circle of family and friends. She lived a life of devotion to her family and to her church. What an incredible woman and what a remarkable life!

Belonged to Eva Lenning – no mark

Belonged to Eva Lenning – very old

A beautiful Noritaki bowl that belonged to Eva Lenning

Intricate necklaces and a bracelet hand made by Eva Lenning and given as gifts

About the Author

Louise Eckhardt is originally from Staten Island, New York City. She completed her undergraduate degree at Wagner College and Masters Degrees at Vanderbilt University and the National War College. She retired from the U.S. Air Force as a colonel and then worked for a major defense contractor. She currently resides in Alexandria, Virginia, and enjoys reading, family history research, and ballroom dancing.

www.ingramcontent.com/pod-product-compliance
Lightning Source LLC
Chambersburg PA
CBHW041612260326
41914CB00012B/1468